The Wild Out Your Window

Also by Sy Montgomery

The Curious Naturalist: Nature's Everyday Mysteries

Journey of the Pink Dolphins: An Amazon Quest

*Walking with the Great Apes: Jane Goodall,
Dian Fossey, Birute Galdikas*

Spell of the Tiger: The Man-Eaters of Sundarbans

For Children:

The Snake Scientist

The Man-Eating Tigers of Sundarbans

Encántádo: Pink Dolphin of the Amazon

The Wild Out Your Window

Exploring Nature Near at Hand

৶৹

Sy Montgomery

Down East Books
Camden, Maine

Cover painting: *The Lamoille* copyright © Gaal Shepherd.

Most of the chapters in this book originally appeared in *The Boston Globe* as part of Sy Montgomery's column, "Nature Journal."

ISBN: 0-89272-575-3

Printed and bound at Versa Press, Inc., East Peoria, Illinois

5   4   3   2   1

Down East Books
Camden, Maine
Book Orders: 800-685-7962
www.downeastbooks.com

Library of Congress Control Number: 2002106605

Yet again, for Dr. A. B. Millmoss

Contents

Introduction

Writing about nature has its hazards. Researching other books, I've been chased by an angry silverback gorilla in Zaire, bitten by ants and chiggers in the Amazon, robbed by an orangutan in Borneo (who then chewed up the interview tapes she had stolen from my backpack), and hunted by a tiger in India. I got dengue fever in Kalimantan, dysentery in Bangladesh, and strep in Laos. Landmines and robbers were a problem in Cambodia.

This book, though, was a piece of cake.

North America is great. You don't have to get shots, snakes don't crawl into your bed, poisonous caterpillars don't drop out of trees, the trees don't exude toxic sap, and, for half the year, there are no mosquitoes. And yet here, you can find creatures, landscapes, and natural phenomena as strange and mysterious as in any jungle.

Beneath your porch, creatures with their skeletons on their outsides and their ears on their knees are singing with their wings. In your back yard, songbirds may be murdering mice, while on your lawn a battle rages between exotic and native species.

All around us, extraordinary dramas unfold daily: bluejays are replanting forests. Baby turtles are launching epic journeys. Voles are warring like gladiators. Plants are eating animals.

And it's getting better all the time—at least in New England, where these essays were originally researched and written as columns for *The Boston Globe*. From beavers to eagles to moose, wildlife once extirpated is now returning to the area, as forests recover from a hundred years of clearcutting, unsustainable farming, and unregulated hunting. This gives us the chance to glimpse animals our parents might never have seen, such as otters and fishers. At the same time, new animals are moving into our area: southern birds are expanding their ranges north. A new ladybug from Asia is swarming into houses. Coyotes are appearing in our fields. It's an exciting time to be watching the natural world, as well as a crucial opportunity: we now have a second chance to save what we nearly destroyed. And that is the ultimate aim of these essays: to urge readers to cherish, savor, and preserve a   natural world brimming with unexpected beauty, drama, and complexity.

Our lives are surrounded by ordinary miracles, everyday mysteries. To find them, all you have to do is indulge your senses. Follow the scent of the earth outdoors on a cool, wet morning in spring. Savor the taste of sundrenched dewberries picked in the wild. On a hot August afternoon, go down to your local pond and inhale the scent of flowering water lilies. On a cool autumn night, let the moonlight call you outdoors to listen for the voices of migrating birds overhead.

In other words, be a hedonist. Look out your window, find something wonderful, turn off the screen you're watching or reading and go outside. You're sure to discover something wholly unexpected. The more you watch, the deeper the natural world will draw you into its mystery and magic.

Sy Montgomery
Hancock, New Hampshire
January 2002

Spring

Moss

First Mercy of the Earth

*T*hey bask in frigid snowmelt like a sunbather soaks up sun on a beach. Before the ferns uncoil, before the tree-buds burst, before the jack-in-the-pulpit thrusts its way through the ice, these humble, tiny plants glow green.

"Meek creatures," as the 18th-century British art critic John Ruskin called them, "the first mercy of the earth," mosses prove again the prophesy that the meek shall inherit the earth, for at the first stroke of spring, the world is theirs. Spring quickens first in the mosses.

Yet those of us who don't know better pass by these lovely plants. Mosses are small and tend to grow in humble places, between the cracks in sidewalks, in the crevices of tree bark, on the underside of rocks. "People don't see them," laments Benito Tan, a Harvard Herbarium researcher who monitors the world's endangered mosses.

Tan admits that he, too, overlooked the mosses at first. As a young botanist in the Philippines, he studied the showier ferns and fern allies, lugging a heavy plant press on his collecting expeditions and returning further weighted down with specimens. An opportunity to study mosses in Canada offered an epiphany: "I quickly found that if I go collecting, I come back with only a small bag. The specimens are so light!"

The mosses' miniature charms won him over. Tan also teaches evening classes for the Arnold Arboretum and New England Wild Flower Society on identifying New England mosses. His message: "Although they're small, they're so beautiful."

A 10x magnifying lens will help you appreciate the lilliputian world of the mosses. Their fanciful common names suggest their staggering variety of form: The humpbacked elves, greenish-black mosses that look like mushrooms; knight's plume, whose light yellow-green feather-like leaves clothe decaying logs; the torn veil mosses of waterfalls; the common hairy cap, the most common moss of Boston woods, named for the hairy, hood-like veil that covers its spore case. It grows in beds that may stretch a hundred feet across.

Mosses evoke the lushness of an entire forest—trees, ferns, vines, bushes, flowers, mushrooms—only in miniature. Most mosses grow only one-sixteenth of an inch to a few inches tall. Yet, in their velvet tapestries, "strength is mingled with humility, gentleness, and charm … reflecting the gladness of wind, sun, and rain," testifies botanist John Bland in his book, *Forests of Lilliput: The Realm of Mosses and Lichens*. "To know them," he writes, "is to feel a nearness to the texture of nature."

Little plants, mosses are little-known. The best-known "mosses" aren't mosses at all. Spanish moss, the stuff that trails beard-like from live oaks in the American South, is not a moss but a bromeliad, related to pineapples. The famous reindeer moss of the Arctic is actually a branching lichen. Irish moss is an alga, and club moss is more closely related to ferns than to mosses.

What are mosses, then? They are, quite simply, a bunch of tiny, leafy stems, growing so closely together that they form velvety cushions. That's it. Mosses have no roots. They have no flowers. They don't make seeds, but reproduce by spores. Mosses lack a vascular system, the tubes that carry water, minerals, and food from roots to leaves in plants like oaks and roses.

"Unlike seed-bearing plants, mosses have not been well-studied around the world," explains Tan. "Because mosses are so small, people thought they were less important." Mosses don't provide food for humans (though none are poisonous, and some animals eat them). Most species adamantly resist taming by cultivation; New Hampshire author and animal behaviorist Elizabeth Marshall Thomas calls mosses "the cats of the plant world." They are largely overlooked in industry and medicine (though, dried, they make great bandages and pillow stuffing).

Relatively few botanists specialize in mosses—but those who do have a rich field to themselves. Not even the most basic scientific inventories of the world's mosses have been completed. Based on published reports and their own collections, Tan and two of his former students just finished compiling a checklist of Massachusetts mosses, some 360 species—perhaps as many as 700 grow in all of New England. At the Harvard Herbarium, "we regularly get specimens sent to us that are new to science" from around the world, Tan says.

For meek creatures, mosses are surprisingly tough. Because their needs are simple, they can grow in alpine and arctic wastes, on bare cliffs, on Main Street, in jungles, in back yards, in bogs. Some grow on bones, on feces, on corpses. One species, naturally luminous, glows in the dark of caves. "Their tasks are enormously out of proportion to their size," observes Bland. "They serve as pioneers carrying life where it could not otherwise be." One very common species, called *funaria*, grows in the ashes of old campfires. A colleague of Tan's recently visited northern California and reported that acres of this species now cover lands scorched by recent wildfires.

This ability to colonize areas unfavorable to the so-called "higher" (or, to be botanically P.C.., "vascular") plants suggests mosses may have been among the earliest creatures to venture from water to land. No one really knows how or when mosses evolved—mosses don't fossilize well, Tan explains. Still, one feels something primal about them, a connection to Creation. Though "in one sense the humblest," Ruskin wrote of the mosses, "in another they are the most honored of the earth's children ... To them, slow fingered, constant hearted, is entrusted the weaving of the dark, eternal tapestries of the hills."

Perhaps this is why a certain Harvard colleague of Tan's reports that he meditates more clearly surrounded by mosses. (So fond did this professor grow of his mossy meditations that he soon found himself ministering to the wild mosses in his yard—including illegally diverting a creek to water them.)

Surely the landscapers of Japan's Buddhist temples knew the value of mosses for soothing the human spirit. Thomas visited a temple in Kyoto last year famous for its moss gardens. Before entering the gardens, though, visitors were asked to meticulously copy, with careful brushstrokes, the two hundred characters of a particular Buddhist chant, "to help focus your mind," she was told, "on the holiness of the place." Only then was the visitor properly prepared to walk outside on the stepping stones that carefully wind through five acres of different varieties of moss. Thomas was deeply moved by the sight. "So soft, so delicate, each stem its own little thing, and all these tiny things joined to become this one great thing—a holy place," she said.

Crazy as a March Hare

৵

As Lewis Carroll was composing *Alice in Wonderland* in 1862, he faced a dilemma: who do you invite to a mad tea party?

A hatter was an obvious choice, for everyone knew what it meant to be "mad as a hatter." In the 19th century, the mercury used in making felt hats caused hat-makers' muscles to jerk spasmodically, like a madman. But not even madmen go to tea parties alone. Carroll had to invent an equally crazy host for the party: the March Hare.

Carroll got his inspiration from an old proverbial expression, "Mad as a March hare." At first, it seems an unfair epithet, at least for our single New England hare species. Most observations of the snowshoe, or varying, hare suggest that for most of the year, it upholds all standards of lapine sanity and propriety. Quiet and shy, the hare is seldom seen except at dusk and dawn, and doesn't cause a ruckus.

But come March, hares go haywire.

Symptoms of insanity appear mid-month: Hares begin to dash about in full daylight, getting into brawls with other hares, engaging in boxing and kicking matches and high-speed chases. In years when there are a lot of hares around "it can be pandemonium—chaos!" says Dennis Murray, a University of Idaho researcher who has studied snowshoe hares in Canada.

And as the month wears on, as Alice might say, things get

"curiouser and curiouser." The strangest scene takes place when male and female meet. Both sniff. Then one leaps over the other (sometimes when one hare is airborne, the other runs beneath it) and the one in mid-air urinates on the one below. Then they switch.

The final evidence of mental instability is that, for the hares involved, this is apparently a huge turn-on. Mating then follows—several times over the course of the next few hours.

For many animals, actually, urine is the flowers-and-candy of courtship. Male goats spray it on their beards like aftershave, male porcupines spray females with it, and male camels, horses, and deer smell and taste the urine of females, sometimes kicking a potential mate until she urinates for him. Urine contains important chemical information about potential mates, including levels of sex hormones. So the snowshoe's courtship performance might not be so hare-brained after all.

Snowshoes can continue acting "mad as a March hare" into September, when the breeding season ends. But you—as were the folks who coined the expression—are most likely to see hares acting crazy in March.

That's because it's the time you're most likely to see hares at all. Rabbits are another matter—and in fact, not just another species, but a different genus. Common cottontails come right up to suburban homes to nibble foundation plantings, and you might spot one any time of year. But snowshoe hares are more secretive, and keep to evergreen woods.

They're built for a tough life. Big furry feet keep them from sinking into deep snow. Long ears help detect predators, from which they can flee at speeds up to thirty miles per hour, including leaps carrying them ten feet in a single bound. (Rabbits, with shorter ears and legs, simply hide from predators and hope they go away.) While rabbit babies are born blind and helpless, hare babies, called leverets, can run within an hour of birth.

And with good reason. "Everyone out there is trying to eat hares," explains John Litvitis, an expert on hares and rabbits and associate professor of wildlife ecology at the University of New Hampshire in Durham. "Bobcats, lynx, foxes, coyotes, hawks, owls—even a weasel can take a hare, and hares don't get much chance to make a mistake." Even red squirrels will kill and eat baby hares, as researchers in the Yukon discovered to their amazement.

Though secretive, snowshoe hares are fairly common from Alaska as far south as California and east from Newfoundland to Virginia. In New England, they're far more numerous now than at the turn of the century, when they nearly vanished. (Because at the same time cottontails were increasing, it was widely believed that cottontails hunted down and killed hares. Actually farmers had mowed down hares' evergreen habitats. Now that the forests have grown back, hares have rebounded.)

In the winter, you can find plenty of evidence hares are around. You'll often see their five-inch-long, triangular tracks in the snow in evergreen woods. You might also find their flattened, M & M–shaped droppings scattered about. (Cottontails' droppings are rounder and left in one big pile.) In a clump of willow or birch, you might see where a hare has nibbled at twigs, buds, or bark—like rabbits, they clip twigs at a 45 degree angle. Beneath a log or amid underbrush, you might even find a hare-shaped depression, or form, where the animal rested, hidden.

But the hare itself is seldom seen—until March. "If you're ever going to see them, now's the time," says Litvitis. The varying coat—brown in summer, white in winter—usually disguises the snowshoe hare so well that, when scent doesn't tip them off, predators walk right past. When Murray was tracking radiocollared hares with telemetry, "I'd be chasing down one hare and another would be right next to me as I was walking by. If it weren't for the telemetry, I'd never have known it!" The only time the camouflage doesn't work is times like these: when the snow has melted but the animal hasn't molted its snow-white pelage.

To race about brawling and leaping in such a vulnerable condition might seem sheer madness. But again the hare's tale grows "curioser and curiouser": producing up to four litters a year drives a dramatic boom-and-bust population cycle. In the northern half of the continent, hare numbers increase up to 100-fold roughly every five years, and then abruptly crash. This is a ten-year cycle that has puzzled and intrigued researchers for decades.

Perhaps most astonishing is that the hare boom is synchronous across the northern four thousand miles of its range, throughout the evergreen forests of Canada. In more southerly climes like New England's, with broken tracts of forest, many different types of predators, and a smorgasborg of alternate prey, most experts agree the hares either do not cycle, or the cycle here is far subtler and more complicated. But we feel the effects nonetheless: the state of hare populations in Manitoba will determine whether there will be extra lynx sightings in northern Vermont.

Up north, the populations of predators like lynx closely "track" the populations of their prey, explains Todd Fuller, an expert on carnivores at University of Massachusetts in Amherst. With lots of hares around, lynx thrive; two years after hare populations peak, lynx populations peak at a 6–10-fold increase. As hare numbers crash, lynx numbers do, too. Hungry lynx may wander widely in search of other prey—and that's when you get lynx sightings as far away from their home range as Vermont and Nebraska.

But the picture is even more complex. Recent research shows that the hare cycle also involves subtle changes in the relationships between plants and animals, parasites and hosts—and perhaps even events on the sun, 93 million miles away.

Among the latest findings about the cycle: as growing numbers of hares begin to decimate the grasses and shoots on which they feed, boreal plants respond by manufacturing new chemicals to make them less palatable. Malnourished hares are more susceptible to parasites like stomach worms. (Weakened, they fall more easily to predators.) And finally, the plant cycle could be controlled by the dark spots on the face of the sun: new work from Canada suggests sunspot activity (a 10.6-year cycle), might affect weather cycles, which could control plant growth, which could affect hare numbers.

"We're starting to realize it's a far more complicated system than we thought," says Murray. "There's a whole lot of factors operating. We're still putting it together."

So perhaps the hare's mysterious March behavior is not madness after all—but an expression of a strategy brilliant and perfect beyond our comprehension.

Vernal Pools

Spring Incarnate

ॐ

*M*ost of the year, they are the places you walk right
past without noticing: The dry bed by an intermittent stream. A depression by the road. A little bowl of leaves in
the woods.

But in the spring, when the world brims with water, such
spots are spring incarnate. They are scenes of metamorphosis
and renewal, where life quickens as if from nothingness, where
silence becomes song, where creatures change from one life-form
to another—and then, come summer, vanish as abruptly as they
came.

These places are called vernal pools. And unless you know
what to look for, you might still walk right past.

In Warner, New Hampshire, naturalist and painter David
Carroll knows what to look for. Visiting vernal pools each
spring is part of a practice he calls "keeping appointments with
the season." For a quarter of a century, as he's studied turtles,
researched books on wetlands, and sought inspiration for his
paintings, he's returned again and again to watch these pools
swell with water and swarm with life.

Here, year after year, in places that look unremarkable and
even lifeless, he finds salamanders as long as your foot, mating in
great squirming congresses, who appear above ground only a few

nights a year and then vanish into the burrows of shrews and voles. He finds the tiny, tumbling, burr-like forms made from bits of hemlock and twig—the carefully constructed camouflage and armor worn by the living larvae of a fly that looks like a moth.

He finds the breeding grounds of frogs that fill the night with the jingle of bells and the sounds of quacking ducks, and the foraging areas of turtles whose shells look like star-studded night skies. "A little bowl of leaves in the woods," he says, "and all this story comes out of it."

Vernal pools, he explains, are temporary worlds, as changeable as the Cheshire cat's grin. "Each vernal pool has its own identity, its own signature," he says. One might be a stone-lined pit where farmers once chilled milk, where wood frogs now breed; another, a boggy-smelling spot along an intermittent stream fringed with sphagnum moss, where female four-toed salamanders guard their eggs. Another might be dotted with hummocks of tussock sedge and canary reed grass that will tower over your head come summer, where spotted turtles hunt for food and seek out mates.

It might seem a different season in each pool. One shaded by hemlocks might still be covered with snow, and even in late spring still contain spotted salamanders; another pool, a mile or two away, will harbor only the gelatinous egg masses from salamanders who left weeks earlier.

Some contain fairy shrimp—wraith-like, inch-long crustaceans so transparent you can see their beating, tube-shaped hearts. They swim on their backs, waving plumes of combined breathing and swimming organs. When the pool dries, only their eggs survive, to hatch the following spring—or years after that, if there's not enough rain. Other vernal pools host freshwater clams who spend most of the year buried in dried-out mud. In some pools, wood frogs will breed one year and not the next, when spring peepers might come instead.

Not only do these places change; part of their definition is that they actually disappear. Another part of their definition is what is not present: vernal pools have no permanent inlet or outlet for the water that feeds them. Many have no water plants, only dead leaves. They can't support fish: they are too shallow, too warm, too oxygen-poor, too temporary.

But as Becky Suomala, nongame program associate at the New Hampshire Fish and Game Department points out, "It's a risky place for animals, but there are a lot of benefits. Because these areas dry up, they don't get predators like fish." That's why so many amphibians—wood frogs, as well as the spotted, blue spotted, Jefferson, and marbled salamanders—lay their eggs only here. Dozens of other species avail themselves of the pools when they can.

Only creatures able to transform into something else would choose such a changeable birthplace. Vernal pools are themselves amphibious. As Carroll explains, the very word amphibian means "two lives." Like amphibians, vernal pools "have this life of water," he says, "when they hold the most life—and then another life, as a dry basin in the forest."

So the creatures who come here are changelings. Mosquitoes transform here from eggs to jerky-wiggling water creatures to the despised winged, biting flies. The caddis fly larvae, as Carroll puts it, "tumble-bumble" about the water in their silk-lined, hedgehog-like camouflage until they pupate and metamorphose into delicate, moth-like creatures with thread-thin antennae and scale-covered wings folded like tents over their backs. Baby salamanders and frogs hatch into gilled, swimming larvae and then grow lungs and legs and crawl or hop away. "Vernal pools are great scenes of metamorphosis of insects and amphibians," says Carroll. "There's nothing like it in the fish, birds, or mammals. This physiological complexity is unparalleled in the vertebrate world."

In some cases, these creatures' behavior is as complex as their physiology. Consider the four-toed salamander. Like all salamanders, it is a creature so aquatic it can swim like an eel; but it spends most of its life out of water, hiding under stones and leaf litter in hardwood forests surrounding boggy areas. But unlike most salamanders, the slender, reddish brown four-toeds don't lay gelatinous masses of eggs in the water. Theirs are laid singly, attached to sphagnum moss, and the female actually guards her clutch—as would a bird.

Bravely the little salamander waits, hidden in the wet moss fringing a vernal pool or stream, for up to a month and a half until her babies hatch. Though she is only two to four inches long, and slender as a newt's tail, she has a secret defense: a constriction at the base of her tail. If a predator attacks, the tail breaks off, still squirming, while she escapes. Later, she will regrow a new tail.

One spring day Carroll found eight of these slender, silver-bellied creatures, hidden in the sphagnum moss surrounding a single vernal pool. Other lives here hide in plain sight: few people imagine caddis fly larvae to be anything other than debris. They don't look long enough to see the shy creatures stick their necks out of their armor or watch their tumbling movements. Most people overlook the fist-sized, gelatinous egg masses of wood frogs, because they don't show up easily in the leaf-stained water. And the few who spot light-colored dots the diameter of a pencil at the bottom of vernal pools generally don't realize these are the sperm packets left behind by spotted salamanders. The gyrating males lead the females to these packages, and by nudging and jinking, try to urge her to pick up one of his to fertilize the eggs in her body.

Vernal pools teach us to look deeply, to appreciate how crucial subtle places can be. It's a lesson we're only beginning to learn. "These kinds of places are lost all the time," says Carroll. "People culvert them, cut trees around them, build driveways over them. This," he said, standing hip-booted amid the boggy, forested wetland of high-bush blueberry, hemlock, and red maple, "is the typical sort of place that gets annihilated when a housing development comes in."

Some states offer no legal protection for vernal pools (though local conservation commissions may be persuaded to protect them.) Other states, such as Massachusetts, allow them limited legal protection as wetlands. But as herpetologist Brian Windmiller has pointed out, saving a vernal pool is like saving a bird's nest: it's crucial to the creatures' survival, but not enough to ensure it. For the animals who use vernal pools often live far-flung lives—lives whose startling beauty, strangeness, and complexity we glimpse there only in spring.

Flowers That Stink

The Many Ways to Court a Pollinator

$\mathcal{S}$ pring stinks.

That's not just a crank's complaint about mud season and black flies. Some of the earliest harbingers of spring are flowers whose fragrance, far from smelling "April-fresh," fills the woods with a revolting stench.

The scent of one species, the aptly-named skunk cabbage, combines the olfactory charms of skunk, putrid meat, and garlic. Henry David Thoreau compared the odor of another species, the carrion flower, to that of a dead rat in a wall. Still others—like the little red and purple trillium—actually look like meat that's gone bad. Some even give off the heat of a putrefying carcass.

It's not the kind of bouquet you'd present to your sweetheart—unless you're courting a fly.

And that's exactly what these early spring flowers are doing.

"Everything about a flower tells you something about its pollinator," says Barbara Pryor, spokesperson for the New England Wild Flower Society's Garden in the Woods in Framingham. These flowers' carrion-like stench are a dead giveaway. They stink in order to attract flies, carrion beetles, and other insects who glory in rot.

Why court a fly if you're a flower? The plant isn't seeking the insect to have sex with it; but a flower may well seek an insect to have sex *for* it. Critters from bats to butterflies can get into the act, too, and if you look carefully at a flower, you might well guess who its pollinator is.

Though plants do move (the Oriental kudzu vine can grow at the horror-movie rate of a foot a day), they can't wander off to get together with members of the opposite sex, like animals do. In order to ferry pollen from one flower to another, most plants must borrow mobility—from wind, water, insects, birds, or mammals.

Wind is the most ancient method for cross-pollination. During the swampy Carboniferous era, most plants were wind-pollinated (and we burn their detritus as coal and oil today). Many plants, from bamboo to pines, still reproduce this way.

But during the Cretaceous period, 144 million years or so ago, a revolution took place. Plants figured out a way to get other living creatures to ferry their pollen back and forth. To secure these creatures' services, the plants had to entice and reward them. The extravagant shapes, colors, markings, and scents of flowers are all advertisements to attract the right pollinator at the right time.

To the plant, a flower can represent a huge investment. Consider the pink lady slipper orchid. The single, five-inch-tall slipper-shaped bloom and its foot-long stalk amount to 15 percent of the plant's dry weight. Studying the orchid and the bumblebees who pollinate it in the hardwood forests of eastern Massachusetts, Boston University's Richard Primack and Pamela Hall have found that the effort of producing the spectacular bloom can tax the plant for up to four years afterwards.

For the jack-in-the-pulpit, a swamp plant that produces a pale, clublike spadix ensconced like a preacher in a purplish-brown, canopied "pulpit," flowering and setting fruit is so exhausting that the plant may switch sex from year to year. Only in years when it has stored plenty of energy in its tuberous root will an individual turn female and produce the tiny flowers hidden at the base of the spadix, which, pollinated by gnats, will develop into scarlet berries. "It's a wonderful clue to see how important flowers are to the plant," says Jorie Hunken, a Woodstock,

Connecticut naturalist specializing in the natural history of plants.

Many flowers are custom-made to attract just one or two pollinator species, and to exclude others. Some plants are pollinated only by beetles. Others court mainly butterflies. Still others (mainly in deserts and tropics) attract bats, mice, and even opossums.

A surprising number of plants are pollinated by flies. Despite their questionable palettes, flies make fine pollinators, and some flowers work hard to attract them. In Borneo there grows an orchid whose hundreds of tiny reddish-yellow flowers emit an odor that has been likened to a herd of dead elephants. In their book, *Ingenious Kingdom*, Henry and Rebecca Northern report that "persons studying the plant in an enclosed place fainted from the overpowering stench." (Even worse is the eight-foot-tall *Amorphophallus titanium* of Sumatran jungles. It attracts carrion beetles with a scent like rotting fish and burnt sugar, and people have been known to pass out from simply walking by one in bloom.)

The smell of skunk cabbage isn't nearly so vile, but as far as flies are concerned, it has an additional draw: warmth. With an oven-like shape and an in-curving, leaf-like spathe sheltering its tiny flowers, the skunk cabbage actually begins to melt the snow around its leaves—as would the rotting corpse of some poor, winter-killed animal. Rotten meat may sound unappetizing, but it's nutritious stuff, and so is the skunk cabbage's pollen: It's exceptionally rich in starches and nucleic acids.

The flies who flock to this odoriferous banquet aren't just the big bluish kinds who frequent untidy butcher shops—there are plenty of tiny, gnat-sized flies, too. Fly-pollinated flowers tend to bloom close to the ground—the sort of place you'd look around for carrion. As a further enticement, the purplish-red blooms of trillium, and the dark-red flowers of wild ginger, also mimic the color of meat that's past its prime.

Color is an important advertisement for a specific pollinator. Many bees prefer blues and yellows (although a group of pigments some flowers produce, called anthoxanthins, look white to us but blue-green to honeybees, whose eyes are sensitive to ultra-violet light.) Big, white blooms show up at night, and appeal to moths and bats. Hummingbirds love red flowers. In fact, Stephen L. Buchmann and Gary Paul Nabhan—scientists who eagerly test their own hypotheses—report in *The Forgotten Pollinators* that red is so strong an attractant, "if you put on lipstick, fill your pursed mouth with wine, and stand where crimson colored sugar feeders or potted magenta flowers have been outside, the hummingbirds will often feed right out of your mouth."

The size and shape of a blossom matters, too, as Hunken points out. Many small, delicate flowers are pollinated by tiny flies—anyone else would be too heavy to land on it. Bumblebees pollinate flowers whose blooms are thumb sized or bigger; the blooms of bluets and toothworts literally dump these big bees off when they try to land, admitting only the small, stingless, native bees. Tube-shaped flowers, like columbines, are perfect for the long tongues of butterflies and moths, but exclude bees.

Wild lupines, like the flowers of peas and beans, have trap-doors, explains Hunken: a bee pushes on the lower lip of its "Dutch-girl" face to enter, and gets brushed with pollen along the way. Mountain laurel flowers work the same way, she says: stamens tucked into pockets "throw pollen onto the bee in a Happy New Year sort of way."

Some flowers have special platforms to make it easier for pollinators to land, like a store might advertise its convenient parking. Native azaleas come equipped with landing pads, "just like the markers you see in an airport," says Pryor. Yellow dots in the center of the petals "tells them right where to land to get the nectar."

But in the plant world, as well as in human endeavor, not all advertisements are truthful. Flowers can lie. The tropical blooms of the Orphrus orchid lure wasp pollinators with false promise. The flowers' shape and feel so perfectly mimic the sex organs of some species of female wasps that male wasps swarm to the blooms to try copulating with them—tricking the insects into fertilizing the flower instead of another insect.

Salamander Rains

*U*p in Warner, New Hampshire, David Carroll is waiting. "It's like the night before Christmas," says the swamp-loving author and illustrator. He keeps his radio tuned to the weather and keeps his hip waders by the door.

Down in Lunenburg, Massachusetts, wetlands consultant Brian Butler is waiting. "It's always a crapshoot," he says. "You just can't say in advance what night it will be."

And over in Lincoln, Massachusetts, Audubon herpetologist Tom Tyning is waiting. "They might be coming this week," he predicts.

They are waiting for one of the most strange and thrilling of North America's wildlife spectacles: the emergence and mass migration of scores, hundreds, sometimes even thousands of glistening, yellow-spotted, jet-black salamanders almost as long as your foot.

The salamanders are waiting, too. They wait, poised, snouts out, at the entrances of the tunnels of short-tailed shrews. Hidden here, usually six inches beneath the soil, they spend almost every other day of the year—which, of course, is why so few people even suspect that the exotic-looking spotted salamander actually lives among us, occupying a third of the continent from Nova Scotia to east Texas.

The salamanders are waiting for the evening temperatures to rise above the low 40s for two nights in a row, and for these conditions to coincide with rain from afternoon into night. This happens as early as January or February in the Great Smokies and the South, and during March or April in the North. Carroll calls these soaking storms "the Salamander Rains"—for they are the signal for these amphibians to leave their tunnels and make the yearly pilgrimage to the shallow, fishless, temporary pools where they spawn.

"You see the magic in one night," says Brian Windmiller, a wetlands consultant based in Concord, Massachusetts. "One night, nothing is going on—and the next night there could be hundreds of animals on the move."

It's a perilous journey. So many salamanders are squashed by cars as they cross crowded streets to reach breeding pools that in Amherst, folks installed special tunnels to funnel the creatures beneath dangerous roads; in Lenox and Framingham, roads are closed and cars rerouted during migration.

If you drive twenty miles an hour and keep an eye out, though, you'll have a chance to see the brightly spotted critters streaming across the road (and avoid running them over). In fact, to make sure you don't miss the migration, area specialists suggest "herp cruising": on rainy nights, drive slowly down streets that wind through woodlands and wetlands. Or walk around with your flashlight. Listen for the duck-like "ruck-ruck-ruck" calls of the wood frogs and the bell-like jingle of the first spring peepers. They will lead you to the vernal pools where the salamanders spawn.

Here, in water usually only inches deep and often still fringed with ice, you may find what is called a salamander congress: "A mesmerizing interweaving of black salamanders with yellow spots, supple and graceful, moving in the water," as Carroll describes it, "like one of Escher's prints come to life."

Hundreds of giant, gyrating amphibians is not the sort of thing that leaps to mind when you think of places like New England or Missouri or Nova Scotia. "They look like something from the tropics," says Butler. You're most likely to see spotteds during the salamander rains, but you may also find rarer species like blue spotteds and brownish-gray Jefferson's salamanders as well.

Though seldom seen, salamanders may be among the commonest critters around: a 1975 study at Hubbard Brook Experimental Forest in New Hampshire estimated that if you took all the salamanders there and weighed them together, they'd outweigh all the other backboned animals in the forest, including all the moose.

How do we know? A few decades back, researchers tried tagging salamanders with radioactive needles and tracking them with Geiger counters. But since radioactive amphibians evoke a certain dread among the general public, Brian Windmiller came up with another idea. He sews little vests for his spotted salamanders, allowing him to outfit each with a lima-bean-sized radio transmitter, permitting him to track twenty-six of them with telemetry.

Fittings are admittedly difficult. Besides being slimy, "these guys have no waists," he complains. (Couture for the frogs was much easier.) Happily for the salamanders, the vests come off easier than they go on: the animals shed their skins every few weeks, and with them, their outfits.

The radio vests have helped Windmiller achieve a startling estimate of the population of his study area: during the salamander rains, some 10,000 amphibians (including salamanders and frogs) pile out of the woods and surge into a single, one-acre vernal pool in Concord. "That's nearly 300 pounds of amphibians," says Windmiller. It's a finding that proves these ephemeral, embattled wetlands, and the land that surrounds them is "the richest, most productive place in the woods."

That this fact comes as such a shock is testament to salamanders' modesty. These shy animals were so little-known that for centuries their mysteries could only be explained by magic. Along with gnomes and nymphs, salamanders were considered one of the "elemental spirits" representing earth, water, and fire, according to the system of 15th-century alchemist Paracelsus. Salamanders were long thought to be born of fire. The idea probably arose because salamanders often live under logs and were sometimes unwittingly transported to home hearths. When the fireplace was lit, distressed salamanders rushed out of the blaze—giving the appearance of having arisen from flame.

Yet the spotted salamanders' true story is more remarkable still. Born not of fire, but spawned on ice, they are offspring of females who manage to emerge from orgies as virgin mothers.

Male spotted salamanders deposit their sperm before they even meet the females. Having littered the bottom of the vernal pool with sperm-bearing capsules, they then wriggle and gyrate, nuzzling and petting every female they contact in orgy-like abandon. Each male's efforts seems to be focused on inducing as many females as possible to pick up his sperm capsules, which she does with short appendages beneath her tail. She lays her eggs in a gelatinous mass shortly thereafter.

"It is a very curious way of going about mating," says Carroll, "but whatever happens, it's obviously very exciting for them and they wouldn't miss it for the world."

Neither would he. Attending the salamander emergence has, for Carroll, become "like a sacred rite," he says. "It's the real way to celebrate spring."

"The preconceived notion is that spring is when the robins come to eat the worms," he continues, "but by then spring's almost over. When these amphibians start to move, the season is on the wing. I can't bear to miss it."

The Little Gentleman
in Black Velvet

॰ঌ৽

*I*n the spring, you're sure to spot a literary celebrity in our
     midst.

With a velvety coat, whiskered snout, and big, cartoon-like
hands, the mole, scurrying across the road, racing through the
grass, or making shallow tunnels in newly dug gardens, looks
just like its famous namesake from *The Wind in the Willows*.

Gardeners and greens-keepers detest the molehills and
tunnels, but the mole itself—soft, small, seeming to squint Mr.
Magoo–like in the sun—is almost irresistibly charming.

"If you ever saw a picture of a mole, or held one in your
hand, any bad thoughts you might have had about moles would
disappear," promises Patricia Guptill, who studied moles as a
graduate student at Indiana State University.

Most of us are blessed with at least three species of moles in
our area, depending on where we live. The eastern mole, found
in southern Ontario and from southeastern Wyoming and Texas
to Massachusetts to Florida, looks pretty much like the standard,
stout, cylindrical, four-inch model with a short, naked tail. The
hairy-tailed mole is found throughout much of the same region,
and is distinguished from the eastern mole by (you guessed it) its
hairy tail. And the star-nosed mole, also an easterner, is unmis-
takable: the tip of its muzzle is ringed with twenty-two pink

fleshy appendages known as tentacles, which this water-loving creature uses to locate prey underground and under water. There are also three species of Western American moles.

Mole populations can triple between May and June, when there may be as many as eleven per acre. At the tender age of ten weeks, males quest after their own territories, often traveling above ground—giving you an extra opportunity to encounter what one book editor has suggested is "perhaps the most engaging of all wild animals." (Bear in mind that this was the editor who wrote the jacket copy for a book on moles, *The Mole* by Kenneth Mellanby.)

But he has a point. Moles are widely admired. For years, the brave English rebels, the Jacobites, commenced their feasts with a toast to a mole, raising their glasses "to the little gentleman in black velvet"—the particular mole who, digging near Hampton Court in 1702, constructed the molehill over which the horse of the despised King William III stumbled. The horse threw the king and he died a few days later.

From detailed probes of moles' underground lives, researchers can now confirm what the Jacobite story suggests: a mole is a force to be reckoned with.

True, moles have no external ears and their eyes are so tiny you can hardly see them at all. (You can make out the star-nosed's eyes if its face is wet from a recent swim, or the hairy-tailed's by gently blowing the fur back from the face. But the eastern mole's eyelids are actually permanently fused.)

But moles are not dim and helpless, as they're often perceived to be. This modest hero of children's stories is a creature of surprising strength, exquisite sense, and, if the situation demands, startling savagery.

"So much is written about the aggressive nature of moles that one might be forgiven for thinking of them as the raging psychopaths of the countryside," assert Scottish mammalogists Martin Gorman and R. David Stone of the University of Aberdeen. Their review of mole literature unearthed many accounts of mole gladiators. One experimenter put a mongoose and a viper together with a mole, and the mole dispatched them both.

Moles will kill and eat other moles housed with them in captivity, and will occasionally bite people who pick them up. (To avoid this, pick up the mole by its tail, or hold its head still behind the jaws. Even if it does bite, you won't get rabies; there's no record of a mole transmitting this disease.)

Fortunately, the average mole faces few such annoying encounters. Under normal circumstances, it behaves like a gentleman, disturbing no one, except for the tons of invertebrates it consumes over a lifetime. While moles are best known for eating earthworms, in some areas they eat almost exclusively lawn grubs, snails, beetles, and millipedes.

"Better garden pest control you couldn't hope for," Guptill says.

Each mole's burrow system consists of several nests and two types of tunnels. With big, powerful shoulders and shoveling hands, moles almost swim through the soft, shallow soil to create their superficial tunnels—the ridged eruptions that wend through gardens and lawns. Breast-stroking, they push the loose dirt up and aside.

They create molehills as they dig deeper tunnels. At depths of 10 to 20 inches, they shear away heavy soil with alternating strokes of their hands, pushing it to a side tunnel that leads to the surface.

As the soilheap is brought to the surface, the new soil erupts over the molehill "like a small volcano in action," in the words of one observer.

How do we know about the underground lives of moles? In large part because researchers have succeeded in gluing radio-transmitters onto their tails. Gorman's and Stone's book, *A Natural History of Moles*, records a Dutch mole digging a record 66 feet in one day (a veritable Holland tunnel) and a workaholic Scottish mole who dug nonstop for $4\frac{1}{2}$ hours. (This was an unusual burst of activity, probably a youngster establishing a territory.)

The deep tunnels are used for years, allowing the architect to live a leisurely life once his network is established. Moles don't dig new tunnels each time they forage, and, in fact, a very active mole territory may have few molehills. They appear only when a new tunnel system is constructed, or when an existing one is repaired or extended.

Moles are amazingly strong. The eastern mole can move 32 times its own body weight, which ranges from 2.3 to 4 ounces. But that everyday feat was far surpassed in 1957 by a golden mole—a native of Africa—in captivity. The two-ounce creature was recorded moving an iron cover in its enclosure; the cover weighed 21 pounds. That's about like a 150-pound man pushing around a black rhinoceros.

And moles move fast. That's partially a consequence of their velvety fur; it offers no friction whichever way it's rubbed, so a mole can sail through its polished tunnel.

(The unique softness of mole fur has fueled several fashion crazes for moleskin coats, but each of these fads faded away— perhaps because the coats develop pressure marks that display all too clearly the anatomical details of the wearer's derriere when they're sat on for long periods.)

You might think that dim-sighted moles, propelling themselves through their tunnels at up to 2½ miles per hour, would regularly blunder into walls. That this doesn't happen is due to the creature's exquisitely sensitive snout, which is covered with thousands of Eimer's organs—named after their discoverer. The star-nosed mole's tentacles provide the most striking illustration.

Under a microscope, each of the Eimer's organs looks rather like a molehill, and beneath each sits a blood-filled bundle of sensory nerves. This provides extremely subtle tactile information.

How subtle? One researcher taught a tame mole to distinguish a jar of food from an empty jar by sensing textures engraved on the lid by two one-thousandths of an inch in width and depth.

The mole's face, tail, and the back of its hands are also endowed with special sensory organs. These hairlike structures, called vibrissae, function like the whiskers of a cat. Each sits upright in a fluid-filled sac, like a straw in a bottle. These hairs can move separately and tell the mole's brain not only whenever he touches something, but also the duration, speed, amplitude, and direction of the hair's resulting movement.

"The mole has a more sensitive sense of touch than any other animal alive," says small-mammal researcher Joseph Merritt, director of the Powdermill Biological station in Rector, Pennsylvania.

A mole's world is a dark and tactile one as rich and wondrous as a dog's world of scent. And to us, just as incomprehensible.

Woodpecking

The Earliest Song of Spring

⅋

*T*he woman called New Hampshire's Audubon Society in desperation. This bird was driving her crazy.

Every morning at daybreak, the creature started hammering away at the metal flashing around her chimney. From the big bill and the black and white feathers, she recognized the culprit as some sort of woodpecker. Yet this was clearly no place for a woodpecker to excavate a hole, nor did any tasty bugs live in the metal. "So what's wrong with this bird?" the caller wanted to know. "Is he just stupid?"

Far from it. Possibly he was a genius. The woodpecker, Audubon volunteer Wendy Christensen explained, wasn't trying to make a hole; he was making music.

The territorial love songs of woodpeckers—among the earliest bird songs of spring—are not voiced, but hammered. Usually the instrument of choice is a tree. But this woodpecker had gone one better: by choosing the metal flashing as his drum skin, the bird had made a technological breakthrough, increasing the range of his broadcast several fold.

Other woodpeckers are catching on. New England's Audubon societies get calls each February and March from distressed homeowners who report woodpeckers banging away at gutters, hammering on metal street signs, percussing loose shingles like castanets. "By the time people call us," says Martha Fisher, who handles callers' questions at Cornell University's Laboratory of Ornithology, "the people are close to shooting the woodpecker."

Remedies for these unwanted concerts range from wrapping your gutters in foam rubber to defuse the noisemaker (causing the woodpecker to abandon it) to tacking long streamers to the house to frighten woodpeckers away. Or, you can just ride it out; they'll usually choose a new instrument inside of two weeks. Happily, most woodpeckers don't hammer on houses, but neither will just any tree do. The birds carefully choose trees of special resonance, often hollow or dry, dying ones. In the spring, you might see a woodpecker ascending a trunk, trying out different spots, playing the tree like a xylophone.

Like songbirds' melodies, woodpeckers' tattoos help them stake out territories, attract mates, and generally synchronize the couple's ideas about nesting. Woodpeckers' drumming may seem monotonous compared with songbirds' tunes, but in some ways drumming is richer: the repertoire of the hairy woodpecker, for instance, includes nine different kinds of drumming; and unlike most songbirds, in which only the males sing, in most woodpeckers, the concerts are co-ed, with both males and females contributing.

And there's a message for us humans in this avian Morse code: for us, the sound can serve as an invitation to spectacles of sound, ceremony, and displays, leading to ringside seats at a spring preview of avian conflict and courtship.

"They're spectacular ," said Lawrence Kilham, who studied woodpeckers for more than twenty years. "Beautiful to watch, easy to see, and easy to tell the males from the females—an ideal thing to study." Kilham, a retired Dartmouth virologist (his license plate read VIRUS), watched woodpeckers at his home in Lyme, New Hampshire, as well as in Florida, Maryland, South Carolina, Georgia, and the tropics. In his efforts to know woodpeckers better, he converted a garage into an aviary for orphaned fledglings, and wired fallen, decayed logs to fence posts in his yard to attract the birds (which worked spectacularly; four downy woodpeckers arrived within days.)

Downies may have been quietly visiting your feeder all winter, if you put out suet. These handsome six-inch birds, with white-spotted, black wings and white streaked faces, are the most common woodpeckers in the east. You may have heard one excavating a roost hole in a dead tree in November, or pecking at bark to get at insect larvae during the other seasons.

But woodpeckers' pecking sounds utterly different from woodpeckers' drumming. Drumming entails bursts of loud, resonant pecks that come so rapidly there's no way you could count them. (Their brains are specially padded inside the skull so they don't get concussions.)

Downies have only six vocalizations, but eight different kinds of drumming, each for a different circumstance. Kilham cataloged them all: Dawn drumming calls for a rendezvous with a life-long mate. A few short bursts of drumming, quickly answered, is a downy asking "Where are you?" and the mate replying, "Over here." Woodpeckers sometimes drum when frustrated, when they can't think of anything else to do, like a person might chew his nails when nervous or irritated. Males drum to invite copulation. Woodpeckers also drum discussions over a nest site; an unhurried duet generally indicates agreement, while a more prolonged series of responses may indicate that one bird is trying to entice the other to reconsider. (In hairy woodpeckers, these duets can go on for more than fifteen minutes.)

You may not hear what Kilham called "whisper drumming," low and brief, till April or so, when the nest hole is nearly complete. But in April and May you are very likely to hear territorial drumming , which can often bring on conflicts involving up to four woodpeckers.

The territories woodpeckers are drumming about imply boundaries, and it was at a boundary between territories, along a dirt road near his house, where Kilham saw two downies performing an extraordinary dance one February. He found that the larger, similarly patterned hairy woodpecker does this, too: "It was always a pair of either species involved, and usually low on the trunks of trees," he wrote in his monograph *Woodpeckers of Eastern North America*. "With heads and bills pointed upward, or even backward, and swinging back and forth like conductors' batons, they jerked heads and bodies while making half-starting motions with their wings." The jerking, he said, reminded him of mechanical puppets. After several minutes of this, the birds would pause, frozen in strained postures. The performance might go on for more than an hour.

What were they doing? Previous observers thought this a courtship dance. But watching carefully, Kilham noted both birds possessed the distinctive red patch on the nape of the neck that in both downies and hairies denotes a male. These encounters, he discovered, are not amorous, but aggressive. They always occur between members of the same sex—females will also fight with other females—while the mates observe the spectacle from a nearby branch. Sometimes during these conflicts, one combatant swoops at the other, occasionally even pulling out some of the rival's black and white feathers—which the victor then holds in the bill, waving it literally in the other's face.

Mostly, though, these conflicts are harmless; everyone seems to enjoy it. Kilham knew two pairs "so eager for encounters on some days that they flew from their roost holes to their common border without waiting to feed ... The displays," he concluded, "were a way of working off steam. I thought of a tennis match, in which both contestants are satisfied to have the boundary, the net, stay where it is. Both play on, spurred by having their mates on the sidelines."

Woodpeckers use taps and drum rolls to agree as well as argue. The red-bellied woodpecker (whose belly is more tan than red) uses slow clear taps to register agreement on a nesting site. Tapping is distinctly different from drumming: the taps come at a countable two to three taps per second, with up to twenty in a burst. The male red-bellied (the red patch on his nape extends up to his forehead, while the female's stops short) begins tapping from within the nesting hole; the female simultaneously taps from the outside. These woodpeckers supplement their percussion with voice: during nesting discussions, both may also call "kwirr," the male pointing his flaming crown to the ground. The red-headed woodpecker (whose whole head, and neck, really is red) also conducts a similar ceremony.

In his classic *A Natural History of American Birds*, the great New England birder of the '20s and '30s, Edward Howe Forbush, recorded how this brilliantly colored and pugnacious bird enlivened his visit to the desolate forest of Naushon Island off Buzzard's Bay one winter: "There, on a cold day in February, with a piercing cold northwest wing rattling the dry branches," he wrote, "a red-headed woodpecker in a sunny nook tapped away as merrily on a dead branch as if summer zephyrs were blowing."

No mere noise could so eloquently evoke warmth and light in the dark of winter. That's the music of the woodpecker's tattoo: Think of it as the drum roll announcing the coming of spring.

Asian Plant Twins

꒐

*Y*ou might feel lost in the forest of signs in Tokyo, but
you'd feel right at home in a Japanese forest. There, the
woods bloom with many of the same species that flower in the
Northeast: mayflower, silverbells, trillium, rhododendron, vibur-
num, jack-in-the-pulpit. Many of the woody plants are the same:
maple, hickory, dogwood, barberry, tulip trees.

Woods in much of Eastern Asia would feel familiar to us
Yankees—far more so than the forests of South America or Europe or even the western half of our own country. So similar are
the plants in our woods to those in eastern Asia that "a sense of
deja vu is experienced by botanists of one of the regions visiting
the other," observes David Boufford, assistant director of the
Harvard University Herbaria, one of the largest collections of
plants in the world.

How such similarities came about is a puzzle that has intrigued and mystified some of the West's greatest minds for two
centuries, and one that today's scientists continue to explore.

Each spring, as hundreds of twin species bloom simultaneously in Eastern Asia and the Northeastern U.S., these plants tell
the history of separated siblings, of epic voyages on drifting continents, of the restless heaving of the earth.

It's as dramatic a story as any in human history—even if it is
played out in slow-motion by creatures we think of as sedentary,
says Judith Sumner, who teaches botany at Assumption College

in Worcester, Massachusetts. "These plants have ridden around the world, been chased by glaciers, cut off by mountains, heated up, cooled down, invaded by northern plants, by southern plants—a wild life! They've been though a lot!"

Carl Linnaeus, the 18th-century Swedish-born naturalist whose classification of species is still used today, was one of the first to wonder at the improbable similarity between the flowering plants of east Asia and eastern North America.

His students were among the early botanist-explorers who scoured the New World and the Orient for strange and marvelous new specimens. On their lists of newfound oddities, the same names kept turning up from both continents: field lily, white pine, juniper, black maple, striped maple, clematis, magnolia, sunflower, witch-hazel, mint ... For centuries, on opposite ends of the earth, ginseng was used as a tonic by both native Americans and Oriental herbalists. The American and Oriental plants are so similar that American collectors exported our version to China.

Why were the plants so similar? Ben Franklin noted that the climates of "the eastern coasts of the old and new continents bear much analogy." Japan and New England, for instance, share similar soils and climates, cooled by sea breezes and tempered by mountains.

That's why Asian transplants, like ginkgo trees, thrive in the northeast. In New York and Boston, horticulturists were quick to embrace Oriental species. You'll find many Asian species growing in Harvard's Arnold Arboretum, and as street trees in New York. At New England Wild Flower Society's Garden in the Woods in Framingham, Massachusetts you can see Asian and New England species flowering side-by-side.

But climate alone can't explain the similarities between the native species of both lands. Our temperate climate isn't unique—but the high proportion of the plants we share only with Asia is.

By the middle of the 19th century, Charles Darwin was grappling with the mystery as he formulated his theory of evolution. "Nothing has surprised me more," he wrote in 1856, "than the greater … affinity (of Eastern American plants) with East Asia than with Western America. Can you tell me whether climate explains this great affinity—or is it one of the many utterly inexplicable problems in botanical geography?"

Darwin asked this question in a letter to Asa Gray, a maverick professor of Natural History at Harvard (and whose wife, Jane Loring Gray, was then president of the organization that would become the New England Wild Flower Society.) Gray had discovered, by carefully comparing plants from both continents, that the two regions share no fewer than 120 genera (a category much broader than species) of flowering plants—forty of which are found nowhere else on earth.

"It would be almost impossible to avoid the conclusion that there has been a peculiar intermingling of the Eastern American and Eastern Asian floras, which demands explanation," Gray wrote in 1859.

The explanation he proposed was revolutionary: that long ago, the plants of these two widely separated areas had shared common ancestors. He proposed that the two lands had been linked by land bridges connecting Alaska and Siberia.

New understandings of the movements of the earth's crust support Gray's ideas. According to the theory of plate tectonics and continental drift, all the continents were once one large mass that slowly drifted into separate pieces, and are drifting still. Fossil plants from Greenland, Alaska, Europe, and Siberia further support the notion. "At one time, when Europe and North America were joined, forests similar to those now found in Japan, central China and eastern North America were continuous throughout the northern hemisphere," explains Harvard's Boufford.

Why, then, don't we have magnolias in Europe or ginseng in Wyoming? As the rafts of continental rock drifted apart, they began to crash into oceanic plates and form mountains. In the American West, the Rockies heaved up and blocked the rain that would have supported the Asian-like forests in much of the central and western part of North America. Many species went extinct.

Later, northern North American and European forests had to contend with the great sheets of ice of Pleistocene glaciers. (In Asia, glaciation wasn't as severe.) In North America, many plants "retreated" south, then recolonized their former range when glaciers melted. But in much of Europe, the Alps and Mediterranean Sea blocked the plants' escape route, and they vanished.

Many of the sibling species that survived on opposite sides of the world retained their family resemblance, but sometimes evolved distinctive new features. The leaves of Japanese maples are more deeply notched than ours. Our witch-hazel blooms in the fall; the Asian witch-hazel flowers in the spring. Our tulip trees grow straight and tall, while China's sprawl.

The changes reflect the demands of their slightly different environments. For instance, American dogwoods rely on birds to disperse their seeds, so the fruits are small and fleshy. In China, monkeys disseminate the seeds, and the Chinese dogwood's fruit is big and round to appeal to primates.

But in China, both the monkeys and the forests are in the throes of another wave of extinction, worse than that caused by the glaciers. Boufford notes that most of China's native forests have been cut to make way for farms and factories and the demands of its one billion people. Far more of our forests have survived—particularly in upstate New York and New England. Sumner agrees: "We're lucky," she says. "Our area is a refuge where a lot of these ancient plants have persisted."

Voles

Klingons of the Rodent World

ॐ

*I*n the spring, if you explore your nearest meadow, you're almost sure to notice tunnels in the greening grass. The biggest tunnels—six inches in diameter—belong to cottontail rabbits. The smallest—an inch or less wide—were made by shrews. The most numerous tunnels, though, are the most distinctive: one quick look and you'll see these 1½-inch-diameter tunnels were created not merely by pushing aside the grasses, but by carefully clipping them from the bottom and sides.

You've come upon the tunnels of the meadow vole, and they lead to a hotbed of sex and violence.

The meadow vole is a cute and chubby one-ounce rodent that looks like a mouse created by a designer of stuffed toys. But don't be deceived. "These are very aggressive little guys," says Luis Ebensperger, who studied voles as a graduate student at Boston University. Voles are the Klingons of the rodent world—ruthless warriors, brave in battle even against unbeatable foes. Researchers who work with voles in the laboratory wear gloves. Graduate students give captive voles names like "Conan" (as in The Barbarian) and "Damien." At the Institute of Ecosystem Studies in Millbrook, New York, small mammal ecologist Richard Ostfeld remembers one male vole who was "so hyper-aggressive he'd have seizures in your hand after trying to bite your finger off." When the vole recovered, it would immediately resume the attack.

Not all voles are ill-tempered; like people, voles are individuals, and some are docile. A good sign that one is not is if it chatters at you. Robert Tamarin, who chairs Boston University's biology department, knows that sound is not a greeting: "What they're doing," he says, "is sharpening their teeth."

Even if researchers weren't plucking them out of their meadows, voles would have plenty of opportunity to use those sharp teeth. They help voles trim tunnels and chew fibrous food, but they also get plenty of use on other voles. Especially in the spring, when vole tempers are short, dangers are high, and passions run hot.

At the end of winter, most voles who survived are living peaceably, sharing communal tunnels and sleeping in groups of up to five in spherical nests of shredded grasses. But spring changes all that. Newly greening grasses, researchers have discovered, contain a natural chemical, 6MBOA, which stimulates the developing sex organs of voles and makes them more aggressive. They fight among themselves, setting territories, and mating promiscuously.

"Voles live fast and die young," says Ostfeld. In the wild, most voles live only about three months before they're killed by another vole or eaten by a fox, cat, snake, coyote, or bird—for many hawks and owls, voles make up 85 percent of the diet. (One feature of vole biology that inadvertently helps out hawks is that these rodents mark their territories with urine, which Scandinavian researchers recently discovered reflects ultraviolet light. Hawks can see UV light—and may well use the voles' territorial markings as signposts to the nearest restaurant.)

But during this short life, a female vole can give birth to three litters with up to nine pink, hairless babies in each. She'll breed again within a day of giving birth. And her babies can begin breeding at the tender age of three weeks—and can continue breeding right into winter.

No wonder vole populations can build quickly. Tamarin's study site, at Audubon's Broadmoor Sanctuary in Natick, Massachusetts, can get so thick with voles that researchers have counted one hundred on a single acre. But, like lemmings—who are just another of North America's twenty or so species of voles—meadow vole populations dramatically peak and crash. For both voles and lemmings, the cycle takes roughly four years. According to Gary Fortier, an Indiana University researcher who has studied both meadow and prairie voles, meadow vole populations rise and fall in synchrony throughout the northern United States. It seems to be a six-year cycle: three years after vole populations last crashed, there could be a big year for voles (after another three years, the population crashes again)—and that's important news for neighbors, from owls to orchardists.

"Voles are very important and well-connected to other species," says Ostfeld. Because they are so aggressive, they drive away other rodents like white-footed mice. Since mice carry the tick that causes Lyme disease, high populations of voles could mean fewer outbreaks of the illness, he suggests.

Voles are important food for other creatures, and their own diet has wide-ranging effects as well: when populations are high and winters snowy, they can girdle enough apple trees to put an orchard out of business. But because voles eat seedling trees, too, they also keep fields from becoming overgrown. They may well keep weed-tree species in check, including the Chinese invader known as Tree of Heaven, whose toxic seeds sprout explosively since mice can't eat them.

Because voles nosh on everything from grasses to forbs to little trees, food probably doesn't drive their population cycles. So what does? The question has intrigued Tamarin for more than three decades; he suspects the key factor may be voles' own nasty tempers.

For reasons Tamarin is still investigating, voles become more aggressive as their densities increase. Males even kill babies before mating with the mothers (who don't seem to hold it against them). Similar outbreaks of violence occur with crowded rats—and crowded humans.

Could studies of voles help humans control our own passions? Tamarin makes no such promise. "We avoid extending our hypotheses to people," says Tamarin. "We haven't even solved the problem in voles yet."

Vultures

Avian Quasimodos

*S*arah Calendar was lowering the blinds of her kitchen windows one evening when she noticed the whirl of dozens of huge wings above the trees in her suburban back yard. As thirty-six eagle-size, red-headed birds settled down to roost in the oaks and pines around her southern Massachusetts ranch house, she ran for the binoculars. She looked them up in her field guide and was astonished: "Who'd think we had vultures over here!" she exclaimed. "It's amazing!"

Some folks might conclude that three dozen vultures in the yard isn't a particularly good sign. In Western movies, at least, a crowd of wheeling vultures usually means that the hero is inches from becoming carrion. Not even Charles Darwin liked the turkey vulture: "a disgusting bird," he wrote, "with its bald scarlet head formed to wallow in putridity."

But for modern bird lovers, the increasingly common sight of these big scavengers is good news indeed. Their Latin name, *Cathartes*, means "cleanser" because that's what they do: clean up tons of carcasses from woods and roads.

Nationwide, the turkey vulture is recovering from the depredations of DDT and misplaced predjudice. Their spread north follows a burgeoning food supply, with the growth of northern deer herds (providing winter-killed carcasses) and the spread of new roads (and their attendant carnage).

Turkey vultures, the most widely distributed vultures in the New World, never bred in Massachusetts until 1954, or in Vermont and New Hampshire until 1979. In Maine, they first bred in 1982. But each spring, thousands of pairs of vultures all over New England sit on eggs, well-hidden in cliffs, ledges, boulder piles, and hollow logs.

Even though their nesting chores, for the moment, take the vultures out of her yard, Sarah Calendar is delighted with the growing vulture population. That's why she's not using her real name, or revealing the town where the vultures roost. Except for a few trusted friends (who she entertains in the bathroom, which offers the best view), she keeps the location a secret.

Vultures are the Quasimodos of the avian world. Though not conventionally beautiful, they possess other graces: soaring effortlessly on teetering wings upraised in a characteristic V, with scarcely a flap they can out-fly even the eagles. One researcher clocked a turkey vulture at 55 kilometers an hour with a 24 kilometer-per-hour crosswind; another recorded a juvenile turkey vulture from Wisconsin that flew 980 kilometers in six days.

And folks who know vultures personally say these big black birds, like the hunchbacked hero, have hearts of gold.

Consider the turkey vulture who now lives at the Blue Hills Trailside Museum in Milton, Massachusetts, a bird of unknown sex named Turkey Vulture. It was raised in the southern U.S. by humans, and given a sneaker to play with as a toy. As a young bird, it had the alarming habit of descending from the skies on six-foot wings to land beside people and chew on their sneakers. The vulture never meant any harm. But, says museum director Norman Smith, "People were getting nervous." It was at that point that the foster family shipped the bird to an animal rehabilitation center, and from there it came to the Museum. Now the bird helps educate museum visitors, tolerating curious crowds with gracious good humor while contentedly perching on a staffer's leather glove.

Then there was Fiver, a hand-raised turkey vulture who lived at the Archbold Biological Research Station in Lake Placid,

Florida in the 70s. He was so attached to humans, he would fly down and run and hop after people, hoping for a head-rub and even trail after their cars. Some of the young researchers at the station nicknamed him Weirdo. (Later he went on to make good, though, acting as the test pilot for equipment such as the radio telemetry that researchers would use in the recovery program to save a more celebrated kind of vulture from extinction, the great California condor.)

These turkey vultures were looking to humans for the same sort of friendship they would expect from other turkey vultures. They are loyal creatures who mate for life—sometimes more than sixty years. They are highly social birds, often gathering in the evenings, outside of nesting season, in large roosts sometimes harboring hundreds of birds. Here, some experts believe, they may exchange information about food sources. They observe what one would call a careful etiquette in vulture culture: at kills they defer to high-ranking individuals, allowing them to feed first.

But even psychologically healthy, wild vultures have habits some people find ... well, unsettling. Their method of self-defense, for example, is to vomit their food, which they can send sailing ten feet. Remember that turkey vultures eat nothing but carrion, and the odor does not improve from the sojourn in the vulture's stomach.

The other end of the vulture can be hazardous, too. Their white legs only look white; it's really "whitewash" from the material they defecate on their legs.

Though these behaviors might distress people, they serve turkey vultures well. Vulture vomit is an effective predator repellent, as researchers who have worked with the species can attest.

Dr. Stanley Temple, Beers-Bascom Professor in Conservation at the University of Wisconsin, was first vomited upon by a vulture when he was fifteen, trying to photograph a female on her nest. (The vomit removed the coating from his new camera lens, but that didn't deter him; he has studied vultures for a living ever since.) Temple insists that "vultures are very clean animals."

They carefully wipe their naked red heads on the ground to clean off any clinging offal. And because a vulture's digestive juices kill bacteria (which is why vultures don't get sick from eating rotten meat), defecating on their legs might even work as an antiseptic wash. It also helps cool them off.

And as far as the turkey vultures are concerned, they smell just fine. They should know. Turkey vultures' sense of smell is highly refined—a rare talent among birds. Ornithologists once thought all vultures found food by sight alone. Even John James Audubon was fooled. In an 1826 experiment, he set out stinking dead dogs and rancid fish, and when turkey vultures failed to flock to the feast, he concluded they had no sense of smell at all. (The problem was his offerings were too rotten even for turkey vultures. They actually prefer relatively fresh food.)

In South America, where many western U.S. turkey vultures spend the winter, the high-flying birds can't see carcasses on the forest floor, because they're obscured by the tree canopy—but they can smell them. Harnessing the birds' olfactory talents, gas companies now pay close attention to vultures circling their lines, for the birds can alert them to the location of leaks.

Turkey vultures' fan club may be small, but it's ardent. Each year in Hinkley, Ohio, the Chamber of Commerce sponsors Buzzard Day on the first Sunday after the Ides of March. Some 30,000 human onlookers flock to the birds' ancestral breeding ledges to welcome about 75 turkey vultures back from their wintering grounds down south. And Temple relates that a wealthy acquaintance of his loved the birds so much that she met with him to try to figure out how to execute her final wish: to offer her dead body to them as food.

Perhaps she figured these high-flying birds could more quickly deliver her to heaven. Turkey vultures can fly even higher than the clouds, so high you cannot always even see them. But if you chance to see a vulture up close, you will notice these iridescent black birds' underwings are a satiny gray. Each turkey vulture, like every cloud, has its silver lining.

Plants That Eat Animals

ॐ

*W*hen first described in 1769, everyone thought it was a hoax. In a letter to Swedish botanist Carl von Linne, Englishman John Ellis wrote of a plant he'd found in the New World whose leaves actually captured and then digested insects.

A meat-eating vegetable? Impossible!

But since Ellis reported the dietary habits of the Venus fly trap, a species confined to the bogs of the Carolinas, some 450 more species of carnivorous plants have been discovered worldwide.

They sound like the stuff of Japanese horror films or heart-of-darkness nightmare jungles (and you can certainly find them there). But what most folks don't realize is that carnivorous plants are, at this moment, probably snaring, murdering, and digesting their prey in a neighborhood near you.

Some lure their victims with promises of nectar, only to drown them in an open pool of acid. Others suffocate their prey in sticky drool, then enfold them in tentacles and finally digest them. Still more lurk submerged in ponds and suck prey up inside special organs, where the unlucky victim is digested.

Don't worry—they're not about to take on anything as big as a mammal. The Northeast's carnivorous plants, which belong to three different genuses, live in bogs and around freshwater ponds, where they feast primarily on flies, gnats, mosquitoes, spiders, and millipedes. They aren't the fearsome giants of the horror movies. No real-life carnivorous plants are—although some grow big enough to capture frogs.

New England's several species of sundews, for instance, seldom grow larger than an infant's pinkie fingernail, and are best observed with a hand lens. Their tentacles are no thicker than a human hair, their minute, club-shaped leaves often overlooked amid clumps of sphagnum moss.

The northern pitcher plant, which drowns its victims, never raises its green and mahogany leaves more than half a foot off the ground. (Its trumpet-shaped, bright-yellow-leaved southern cousins can tower two feet or taller.) Bladderworts, the kind that suck prey inside blister-like organs and then dissolve them, stay underwater, where they can pass for any old water weed.

But, as all predators know, it often pays to appear small and harmless. The better to snare you with.

"They're so deceptive," said Barbara Pryor, spokeswoman for the New England Wild Flower Society. At the Garden in the Woods, we stopped by a patch of northern pitcher plants, whose bowl-shaped leaves gaped like mouths in the bog section. "They look like they're shouting, 'Come to me!' Then they swallow them up and eat their soft body parts—Oh my God! What an adaptation!"

The open maw of the northern pitcher is singing a silent siren song. The leaves produce scented nectar to attract passing flies, centipedes, and ants. But it's all a ruse. The victim who alights on the lip of the leaf discovers, too late, that the free lunch is literally on him.

The upper portion of the inside of the leaf is lined with slippery, loose wax (you can feel this if you put your finger inside. Go ahead—it won't bite). With each step of its little hooked feet, as the insect tries to gain a foothold, it creates a microscopic avalanche of wax and slides deeper and deeper towards its doom.

Next it enters a zone of downward-pointing hairs, so it can't climb out. Finally the struggling insect falls, exhausted, into a pool of diluted enzymes, which digest all but the hard body parts—the external skeleton, the jaws, the lenses of the bug's eyes.

"It's like a stomach inside," notes George Newman, a hospital pathologist who surveys some hundred such gaping stomachs each time he looks out his front door. Much of his front yard in Bedford, New Hampshire is bogland, which is where carnivorous plants generally live—and why they catch bugs in the first place.

Bogs have nutrient-poor, acidic soils. Carnivorous plants supplement this spartan diet with the body fluids of their prey. Although most carnivorous plants could live without meat, those that do catch prey tend to thrive best.

To accomplish this predatory feat, these plants' leaves have evolved to serve not only as photosynthesizing organs, but also to work as traps, tentacles, and stomachs. These systems can be quite elaborate.

Bladderworts, for instance, have evolved blister-like catching devices on their grasslike, underwater leaf blades, equipped with feeler bristles and closed with a cover. When a tiny crab or insect larva touches the feeler bristles, the cover snaps open inwards, and with the inflowing water the prey is swept inside to be digested.

So animal-like are carnivorous plants that it's easy to forget that they also possess vegetative talents. "People are amazed that they flower," said Rob Gardner, curator of a famous carnivorous plant collection at North Carolina Botanical Garden at Chapel Hill. Some carnivorous plants boast only inconspicuous flowers. But the northern pitcher plant showcases some of the strangest and most beautiful forms in the plant kingdom.

They look like flowers from Mars. They don't seem to be the right color: an unearthly bronze or mahogany, much like the hungry leaves (the leaves are also often green). Atop a tall, stiff stalk, the peony-like bud bends down as June approaches. When the bud unwraps, five petals expand to hang down like flaps of silk around a hollow, snout-like affair. Beneath the snout hangs a thing that looks like some kind of shield. The whole effect is like a daffodil on drugs.

This strange design has a twofold purpose: to attract bumblebees bearing pollen from neighboring plants, and to prevent an individual plant's pollen from fertilizing its own ovary. The weird-looking shield is actually a part of the plant called the style. It provides a convenient landing pad for bees, and together with its interior design, routes bees in a manner that first delivers foreign pollen to the ovary, then picks up a new coat of pollen to be carried to another bloom. Although the petals fall off in July, the rest of the flower remains standing till fall, as the seeds ripen inside.

As Newman's front yard is ablaze with blooms each June, his back yard and greenhouse are full of some five hundred other carnivorous specimens, both local species and others from around the world. Most of them he has grown from seed—a rare feat, as these plants are notoriously difficult to cultivate. For their beauty, their drama, and their rarity—many are declining because collectors illegally dig them up from the wild—Newman has been fascinated with carnivorous plants for nearly five decades.

He remembers his first sight of a wild carnivorous plant as clearly as most of us remember our first date: he was on a Boy Scout trip in upstate New York. He found it growing on a log by a beaver dam. It was a sundew, he remembers. And its sticky little leaves captured his heart.

Charles Darwin had a similar reaction. His first encounter with a sundew, on a heath in Sussex, England in 1869, sparked years of research on these pixie-sized plants. He experimented on them. He fed them milk, eggs, cheese, and soup, poked them with needles, bathed them in chloride of gold to make them drool.

He found the plants exquisitely sensitive and discerning. They could sense and respond to a particle of human hair eight-one-thousandths of an inch long, yet they ignored both the impact of fallen drops of water and getting poked by a needle. "It appears to me that hardly any more remarkable fact than this had been observed in the vegetable kingdom," Darwin wrote in his book on the subject, *Insectivorous Plants*, in 1897.

Sundews' tiny round leaves are covered with even tinier red hairs, at the tip of which you can often see a drop of fluid glistening like dew in the sunlight. But don't be fooled by this innocent appearance. The hairs are the plant's tentacles, and the fluid is its drool.

The drool smells sweet and attracts small insects, who become stuck in it. The tentacles then react: in a slow-motion version of the Venus fly trap's snap, the tentacles bend over the victim, enfolding and suffocating. After the insect has died, the leaves secrete protein-decomposing enzymes that digest the insect's soft body parts. When the sated leaf unfolds, only the hard husk of the bug remains. The skeleton blows away in the wind, and the dewy leaf awaits its next victim.

Summer

The Watchable Woodchuck

ॐ

"It is said that for every creature on this Earth there is a purpose," begins the lead article in the newsletter of the New England Pumpkin Growers Association. But editor Hugh Wiberg clearly doesn't believe it. "Someday, maybe," he writes, "someone will explain to me the 'purpose' of woodchucks."

To Wiberg, the woodchuck, like the despised squash vine border beetle, is simply one more obstacle standing between him and the 1,000-pound giant pumpkin of his dreams. Similar dark thoughts plague gardeners of more ordinary ambitions during the summer, as ripening vegetables disappear and woodchucks, coincidentally, grow rounder and rounder.

In July, woodchucks begin to accumulate the half-inch layer of fat that will sustain their winter hibernation. A particularly hungry woodchuck in a single day may eat the equivalent of one-third of its body weight. Since a big 'chuck can weigh fifteen pounds, that's quite a chunk out of a prize-winning pumpkin.

And then there are the woodchuck holes. With entrances six inches across, the burrows run 25 to 30 feet long and plunge 2 to 5 feet deep. Digging one involves the removal of 700 pounds of subsoil—and the cavity left behind can topple a tractor driving over it.

The woodchuck, it is said, "eats to give himself the strength to dig holes, then digs holes to give himself an appetite."

None of which endears him to gardeners or farmers. But

farmers made the woodchuck the ubiquitous animal that he is—the most frequently seen big mammal in most of the northeastern United States.

Prior to the arrival of European settlers, woodchucks weren't particularly numerous, kept to the woods, and were generally admired. The Eastern Abenaki Indians of present-day New England considered the woodchuck their maternal ancestor, a wise grandmother who taught them to fish, hunt, and build canoes.

But as European settlers cleared their wooded territory, woodchucks adapted. Because farmers planted plenty of food, and also exterminated most of the woodchucks' natural enemies—wolves, cougars, and lynx—the animals thrived in the new, open habitat. Today, with their only predators hawks, dogs, people, and cars, their numbers can reach as high as thirty-nine per square mile.

Even though they brought the population explosion on themselves, the invading farmers declared war on woodchucks. In 1883, New Hampshire established a Legislative Woodchuck Committee, pronounced the animal "absolutely destitute of any interesting qualities" and set a bounty of 10 cents an animal. Other states followed suit. Today there's no bounty, but the war on woodchucks continues.

Naturalist Meade Cadot thinks it's time to rehabilitate the woodchuck's reputation. First, he'd just stop calling the critter a woodchuck—or even groundhog, of February fame. And no, he isn't suggesting it go by its other name, whistle pig—a moniker bestowed in honor of the shrill whistle the fat creature can emit when alarmed. "Really, it's a marmot," says the Antioch/New England Graduate School professor. And marmots are not varmints, he says.

The woodchuck, whose Latin name is *Marmota monax*, is one of North America's five species of marmots. Marmots are members of the squirrel family, albeit exceptionally fat ones. The other marmots all live out west, not in fields but in the mountains. There they enjoy a respectable reputation as "watchable wildlife."

The eastern marmots, if they aren't eating your garden, are just as engaging to watch.

Ask Genie Ferguson, the booking agent for Drumlin Farm Wildlife Sanctuary's three woodchucks. They make public appearances at area schools, camps, and nursing homes for Traveling Audubon Ark's wildlife education programs in Massachusetts. "All three woodchucks are booked every day," Ferguson says—some twice a day.

"Kids think they're adorable, like a giant guinea pig or hamster," says Diane Barker, caretaker to the stars at the sanctuary.

And if the Audubon Ark doesn't stop at your neighborhood, it's likely that wild woodchucks will. You'll see them foraging at the edge of fields, nibbling the grass along median strips, chomping on dandelions and daisies at parks. Sometimes you'll see one holding a choice morsel in both hands, like a child clutching a big apple. You can watch them wash their faces with their dexterous, long-fingered paws. During the warmest part of the day, you might see one basking in the sun, or sleeping on a stone wall, a fallen log—or atop a fence post.

Woodchucks are surprisingly good climbers. They can scramble over fencing as well as burrow under it, and they can make their way up low trees to get fruit. They can swim, too. But in late spring and summer, food is so abundant that athleticism is seldom called for—other than to periodically stand on hind legs for a better view. In this position, many observers have remarked, the groundhog looks like a portly senator about to make a speech.

A woodchuck seldom ventures more than fifty yards from its burrow. Each adult has a summer and winter burrow, some of them with three to five entrances (sometimes called plunge holes.) In fact, 'chucks are the architects of most of the big holes you find in woods and fields. Fastidious housekeepers, they renovate burrow entrances several times a week. Evidence of fresh digging indicates a burrow is occupied.

Another sure sign is an angry 'chuck rocketing out—so don't go poking around in there. It's best not to annoy a woodchuck, as certain dogs and other woodchucks can testify. (A missing tail is often evidence of a run-in with another male. Rivals try to grab the opponent by the tail and flip him over, and often bite the tail off in the process.)

Unlike other marmots, woodchucks don't live in big colonies underground. Rather like suburbanites, they live in single-family burrows. Some researchers have reported finding two-parent households, but family usually means mom and four to six children—until mom abandons the kids or drives them off.

That happens all summer, so there are lots of little 'chucks on the move, looking for abandoned dens to renovate or a new spot to dig their own.

"They have lots of individual personality," says Janet Wright, a mammalogist at Dickinson College in Carlyle, Pennsylvania. "Some are real sweeties, some are very nervous, some are aggressive." She knows this first-hand, because she's live-trapped hundreds of them, spraying each with a different color pattern for easy recognition. (Trapping is no problem, she says: if you're trying to get rid of one that has been plundering your garden, just put a Hav-A-Hart trap at the mouth of an active burrow hole, then release the captive at least five miles away.)

Wright is studying woodchucks' social structure and how this might affect their susceptibility to disease, but she has also pondered a more pressing scientific question: "How much wood would a woodchuck chuck, if a woodchuck could chuck wood?"

For the answer, she consulted a student whose interest lay in the shapes of the muscles of mammals. The woodchuck's limbs, he reported, are adorned with exceptionally strong muscles for pulling back, but not great for throwing forward.

Wright's conclusion: "If they're going to chuck any wood at all," she says, "they're going to chuck it backwards."

Monsters at the Pond

Predaceous Diving Beetles

𝒜 t the edge of the pond, where the mud is soft and warm, where tadpoles and newts dart among the flowering pickerel weed and frogs grin up from the shallows, an innocent-looking brown beetle, its Volkswagen shape neatly adapted for life in water, oars gently through the water with blade-like legs.

Don't be deceived by the benign appearance, cautioned Mt. Holyoke zoologist Ann Haven Morgan. "Although no insect looks more gentle and satisfied," she observed in her 1930 *Field Book of Ponds and Streams*, "none is more fierce and voracious."

In ponds, in pools, in the sidewaters of streams, legions of these beetles seize and gobble up almost anything that moves. Not just mosquito larvae (though they eat these by the dozen). Not just dragonfly larvae (ferocious predators themselves). These things eat salamanders. They eat fish. They eat tadpoles. Not even adult frogs are safe from the predaceous diving beetle.

But wait—aren't critters with backbones—like fish and frogs—supposed to eat bugs, and not the other way around?

"This isn't the way we think the world is supposed to be," observes Robert Roughley, an entomologist at the University of Manitoba. But the predaceous diving beetle defies the rules of the vertebrate world. It "breathes" through its back end, carries its own air supply like an aqualung beneath the water, and can fly as well as dive.

Good thing they're not any bigger. (Fortunately they nip you only if you bother them—or one gets stuck in your bathing suit.) There are some five hundred different kinds of predaceous diving beetles in North America, and the largest grow to an inch and a half—still a relative giant among insects (after all, the average insect is only $3/25$ of an inch long).

There's only one predator in the pond more fearsome than an adult predaceous diving beetle: a baby predaceous diving beetle. The beetle's larval form, called a water tiger, can grow three inches long. It looks sort of like a shrimp, with a head borrowed from somebody's nightmare. Sickle-shaped, hollow jaws clutch its prey and funnel flesh-digesting drool into the victim, till the water tiger literally sucks it dry. It can eat twenty tadpoles a day.

"You can see various science fiction stories were inspired by these," says Donald Chandler, professor and curator of zoology at the University of New Hampshire. "You just know the scriptwriter has seen them." The life of this creature is weirder yet—a real-life sci-fi episode that has lasted 180 million years, now playing at a pond or stream near you.

Northern New England is one of the predaceous diving beetle capitals of the world. More individuals of more different species are found along the 49th parallel, where the U.S. and Canada meet, than anywhere else on earth, even the tropics. Here you may find ten to fifteen different species of predaceous diving beetles in an area of pond the size of a tabletop. (It's hard to tell the species apart, though: with beetles, this is accomplished by looking at differences in the male's genitalia, which sport all sorts of uncomfortable-looking protuberances. Unfortunately—at least for entomologists trying to classify them—male predaceous diving beetles lack these embellishments.)

Yet at least one species appears to be missing: the elusive diving beetle. Last seen by Phil Darlington, Harvard Museum of Comparative Zoology entomologist and biogeographer, at his Rumney, New Hampshire summer house on April 22, 1926, the elusive beetle remains true to its name, despite Chandler's attempt to rediscover it one recent spring, as part of the New Hampshire Globally-Historic Insects survey.

Any species of predaceous diving beetle can provide that "sweet sensation of horror," that "shivery fascination with monsters" that so delight the likes of E.O. Wilson and his entomological colleagues. To see for yourself, go watch the shallows at a pond or pool where the water's clear but also sports some vegetation, where the beetles like to hunt. Watch the top two inches of the water for movement. In a few minutes you may see a black or brownish black beetle, sometimes outlined with dull yellow, floating up backwards to the surface. Then it will lift its wing covers, collect a silver bubble of air, and dive again. This is how the beetle replenishes its air supply.

The beetle can stay underwater many minutes because it carries this air bubble like a diver's air tank. But, for some species of diving beetle, it functions even better: for those who carry the bubble at the tip of the abdomen, the trapped air actually acts like the gill of a fish. As the beetle consumes the oxygen from its bubble, dissolved oxygen from the water diffuses into the bubble to replace it. In this way the insect extends its air supply. And this is fortunate, because the beetle does its best work beneath the water—hunting, eating, mating, and even grooming itself there.

The beetle's toilette brings to mind a sunbather applying tanning oil on the beach—except it's all done underwater. To keep themselves free of bacteria and fungi, these beetles exude two drops of bluish-white fluid from the area near their wing covers, and then rub it all over themselves with their legs and antennae. It turns out this stuff is a steroid compound that also helps them break through the surface tension of the water as well as repels would-be predators. Roughley discovered this last feature when he was moving beetles around with an aspirator and mistakenly sucked one into his mouth. He reacted like a fish would and spat it out— but too late. His mouth was already numb from the chemical.

A better way to move these animals around is with a net. If you take some home in a bucket, you can watch them in an aquarium. But make sure the aquarium has a lid, advises

Chandler. Otherwise, the beetle will fly out. (Many of those pings that hit your windshield in April are predaceous diving beetles, having just emerged from deep ponds where they groggily spend the winter. When they wake, they mate and then fly, looking for the glistening surface of a warm, sun-reflecting pool—which to a beetle's eye looks exactly like the surface of a shiny car.)

The larvae, who are wingless, make better aquarium pets. One caveat: don't put anyone else in the tank if you ever want to see them again. Chicago nature photographer Jim Rowan found this out after collecting a water tiger along with a bunch of other aquatic organisms, including some baby salamanders he planned to photograph. "I was doing fine, photographing the salamander larvae," he said, "until all of a sudden the water tiger started eating them."

Normally the water tiger waits for its prey, reared up like a cobra with mandibles open wide. But occasionally the predator gets impatient. Yves Alaire, a specialist in water tigers at Laurentian University in Ontario, saw a water tiger stalking a caddis fly larvae. These larvae live at the bottoms of streams inside little cases they build from pebbles, sticks, or leaves, which they cement with their own saliva. The water tiger usually sits on the case and waits till the caddis fly pokes its head out, then bites the head and shakes it free. But one time, he said, the caddis fly wisely refused to emerge—so the water tiger bit right through the caddis fly's case and killed it in its own home.

What force could stop such a fearsome predator? Another predaceous diving beetle. They're so predaceous that both the larvae and adults will eat each other. Only one other creature can match their appetites, and that's humans. Predaceous diving beetles can't eat us—but we can eat them. In China (and in Chinatowns around the world), folks collect these beetles beneath streetlights, pull off the legs, wing covers, and head, fry them in oil, season them with salt, and eat them like nuts.

Alpine Wildflowers

Heroic Survivors

*W*hile summer blooms in most of the country, among the windwept, rocky landscapes of New England's alpine regions, spring will be just dawning—and awakening some of the rarest plants in the world.

They live in New England's islands of tundra. They are relics stranded from the retreat of Ice Age glaciers. They are survivors of some of the most severe and unpredictable weather on earth. They "cling to a thin zone of life between rock and sky," New Hampshire Natural Heritage Inventory Ecologist Daniel D. Sperduto writes in *Conservation Notes of the New England Wild Flower Society*, "a small, harsh world of surprising diversity and beauty."

Some species are breathtakingly beautiful. The Lapland rosebay's deep-magenta flowers are colorfully conspicuous on the few spots of windswept mountain ranges in the White Mountains and Katahdin region of Maine where they bloom. Lapland diapensia forms extensive mats of lovely, milk-white flowers. The yellow-flowering arnica, though globally rare, forms great carpets of daisy-shaped flowers in high mountain ravines.

Other alpine rarities are easy to miss. Some, like the cushiony, pink-flowering moss campion, are so tiny they put forth their blooms on stems less than an inch high. Others are so scarce that, until recently, botanists would travel to one of the few spots on earth where they grow and find nary a one: as late as 1991, only five known individual Robbins' cinquefoil plants, with quarter-inch flowers like miniature buttercups, had been identified in the entire Franconia Range of the White Mountains of New Hampshire. The only other place on earth where this diminutive member of the rose family grows is the Presidential Range, also in the White Mountains.

And yet other rare alpine plants are so subtle you need a magnifying glass to appreciate them: the elfin, white snapdragon-like flowers of Oakes eyebright—known from only two locations in Maine and New Hampshire—grow only two inches high and are hidden among the leaves.

"Many of these species are not all that showy," says Bill Brumback, Conservation Director of Framingham-based New England Wild Flower Society, "but when people hear the stories about them, they become really excited."

Their stories are intimately linked to the forces that created the mountains on which they survive. They are products of the heaving and folding of the earth's crust, the drifting of continents, and the growth and retreat of great glaciers.

Their history explains why many of these plants are so rare: the habitats in which they survive—mountain tops, wind-blown ridges, heath barrens, alpine stream banks—are remnants of tundra that once covered much of New England twelve thousand years ago.

As the great glaciers receded, they left in their wake a broken, rocky landscape of exposed limestone and marble, stripped of most of its soil. Spruce trees, which had survived in the south, eventually recolonized much of this area, shading out understory plants and acidifying the soil with dropped needles. As the climate warmed and the spruce forests covered first the valleys and then the lower and middle slopes of mountains, the tundra plants were left stranded on New England's highest peaks.

Today, these plants are heroic survivors. In winters of the past thousands of years, they have withstood temperatures that can plunge to 40° below freezing, winds that rage up to 230 miles-per-hour, six months of drought, and some of the thinnest, poorest soils on earth. Blowing snow and sleet scour these mountains like sandpaper; in spring and fall, the soil can freeze and thaw daily. Summers on these peaks are no picnic, either: Mt. Washington boasts only thirty frost-free days a year, and the hottest summer day gets no warmer than 70°. Even July can bring freak snowstorms, gale-force winds, and sheeting rain.

These extraordinary forces sculpted extraordinary adaptations. Many of these plants are dwarfed to avoid the deforming, dehydrating force of mountain winds. A rare species of alpine blueberry, for instance, grows only three inches tall. Boott's rattlesnake root (named for a related plant's use against snakebite by Native Americans) is "a giant of the alpine world," says Chris Matrick, Rare Plant Curator at New England Wild Flower Society; it grows 10 to 12 inches tall.

But most alpine species hug the ground, and sport thick, small, leathery leaves to conserve water. Some can even convert the sun's light to energy at astonishingly low temperatures and light levels.

Yet, ironically, the footsteps of hikers may threaten these tough survivors today. Their existence is so precarious, "it doesn't take much to wipe out these plants," says Brumback.

The tiny Robbins' cinquefoil, for instance, was nearly eradicated by its admirers. Once the species was discovered in 1824, overzealous collectors pounced upon the tiny plants, removing perhaps a thousand of them from their last refuge in the White Mountains. Probably the rarest plant in New England, it was once so sought-after it was sold in Boston for 10 cents a plant. Hikers along the Crawford Path to Mount Washington (now part of the Appalachian Trail) ran directly through the heart of its prime habitat, a stony, barren-looking field of only two acres.

"Unless it's in flower, it's relatively easy to just walk right over it," said Ken Kimball, research director for the Appalachian Mountain Club, which re-routed this trail and another to protect the plant between 1979 and 1983. Because the plant is so inconspicuous, though, it was still vulnerable: twice since the plant was federally protected as an Endangered Species, helicopters—one a commercial venture, another belonging to the Army—have landed directly on the Robbins' cinquefoil patch. "Had there been a mishap, like a crash or a fire, it would have been a catastrophic event," said Kimball.

That's one reason why the Appalachian Mountain Club, the Wild Flower Society, and other conservationists considered it essential not only to protect the existing patch but also to establish several other patches elsewhere. In cold frames and carefully tended plots at the Framingham Garden in the Woods, Rare Plant Curator Matrick runs a Club Med for New England's beleaguered plants. "Because they're growing here, they're far more advanced than plants of the same age growing up there," he explains. In the wild, Robbins' cinquefoil takes twelve years to mature; at the Garden, it may flower in only two. For nearly a decade, the Society has grown and transplanted several hundred Robbins' cinquefoil plants, returning them to places where they had vanished.

Careful stewardship of the Robbins' cinquefoil has been so successful that the species joins the bald eagle among the twenty-seven federally protected species proposed to have sufficiently recovered to be taken off the endangered species list—"a success story," says Kimball, "that is moving ahead. What's come out of this is we've learned from this plant how to understand and manage other alpine species."

An exhaustive survey compiled by the New England Plant Conservation Program, which Brumback administered, revealed that 20 percent of New England's three thousand native plants are at risk of disappearing. Thirty-three of them are alpine species.

Only thirteen square miles of alpine habitat survive in the entire Eastern United States today. "The species we have there are rare and unique," says Brumback, "and they are representatives of rare and unique places we have a responsibility to conserve."

A Riverwalk
on Cobble and Sandbar

🦋

*T*he stones of the riverbed appear arranged by a Zen artist. Pale pink, deep brown, dusky blue, with diamond-like glints of mica here and there, each stone has been polished to silken smoothness. Like letters in a word, they seem to spell out peace.

Spring's raging floods may have been stilled months ago. Yet, in the hot grip of a summer drought, along these placid cobblebars you can still see the wild force of ice and flood.

Cobblebars, explains David Carroll, are "the rock collections the river keeps." (Cobbles, technically, are water-smoothed rock fragments three to ten inches in diameter. Smaller rocks comprise gravel, sand, or mud; larger ones are considered stones or boulders.) A Warner, New Hampshire–based naturalist, artist, and author, Carroll has been walking wetlands for five decades, since he was a boy, chronicling the lives of swamps, rivers, bogs, and pools in books, sketches, and paintings. Along cobbled waterways, he can read the dramatic stories sculpted by "the great depth and wild force of the swirling whitewater currents that rage down the river," as he writes in *Swampwalker's Journal: A Wetlands Year*. In the stones, banks, and plants of sand- and cobblebars, he sees "testimony to the crushing, cutting impact of blocks of ice swept along on the forceful floods of winter's fitful transition to spring."

"Summer is the best time of year," says Carroll, as we begin our walk along the Lamprey River in southeastern New Hampshire—the first river in the state to receive federal Wild and Scenic designation, thanks in part to Carroll's documentation of its graces. As we descend the bank, down from a highway bridge, we're briefly pursued by car and truck noise. But soon other sounds claim our senses: the rushing of water, the song sparrow's exuberant burble, the whirr of katydids.

Walking a river, Carroll says, is more intimate than canoeing it. You see deeper and slower at a walking pace. And thanks to summer's low water, you can walk in a river, not just alongside it. There's no better way to spend a hot summer day than calf-deep in cool water.

"Now, the water is low and inviting and you can cover parts of the river you normally can't reach," he says as we ease downstream, carefully stepping on the slippery cobbles along the riverbed. Happily, walking in a river is one of the most bug-free spots you can find. In the thickets you'd be assailed by biting insects, but fast-flowing waters are patrolled by mosquito-eating dragonflies and their delicate relatives, the damselflies. Gossamer-winged creatures with lyrical names like ebony jewelwing and violet dancer, they float and dance on puffs of air above the water and alight on the outposts of stems.

You wouldn't see these damselflies along the muddier streams where animals like muskrats are found. "These sand and cobble washes are very different," Carroll explains, because the cobbles provide an uneven substrate that creates oxygen-rich riffles in the water. "Most streams have little vegetative growth, or life of any kind in the actual riverine corridor. The life is along the banks. But in summer, in the riffles, you'll find lots of life."

These waters offer habitat for wild trout, wood turtles, smallmouth bass. You might find black and wood ducks passing through, kingfishers, and great blue herons. Insect larvae hatch in these waters, and in nearby backwaters, tadpoles transform into toads. You'll find beds of velvety algae and long green strands of water celery waving in the current, sometimes stretching six feet long. Watercress and water crowfoot grow here, too.

In winter and spring, these plants' roots are under six feet of raging water. Few plants can survive such extremes—a hardiness also evident in the shapes of the plants growing at the river's ice-scoured margins. A tiny island of bluejoint reed grass grows in a pocket of nutrients caught between cobbles, its grasping roots twisted like a gymnast. "You can see how the water has shaped its rooting," Carroll points out. "You can infer the rushing of the water from its shape."

Many of the plants of the floodplain are now in spectacular bloom: blossoming among the cobbles, as if planted by some gardener are crimson cardinal flower; white boneset; blue vervain, with its V-shaped spikes of quarter-inch-deep purple flowers; lance-leaf and rough stemmed goldenrod; and pink steeplebush, with flame-shaped blooms like the garden plant, astilbe. "Look at this for a botanical garden," says Carroll, pointing to a plant community that has somehow anchored on a rock by a riffle dropping into a pool. It has formed a foot-wide island of fragrant wild mint accented with sprays of sedge, embroidered by blue-flowering skullcap and crowned with lavender-flowering Joe Pye weed.

All of them are adapted to the river's bite, and survive here by becoming bonsai versions of their usual selves. In rich, wet meadows, many of these plants would dwarf a man: Joe Pye weed can easily grow seven feet high. But here, it seldom reaches more than seven inches tall. "These plants reflect the river's giving and the river's taking away," writes Carroll in *Swampwalker's Journal*. For here, "enriching detritus is washed away; where tall plants grow, nutrient laden deposits are laid down, flood after flood."

Trees respond similarly to the cycle. Out of the flood's reach, the alders are 12 to 15 feet high. But here, points out Carroll, on the opposite bank, they are only four feet tall. Further downstream, we find the severed branch of an alder that's been chewed by a beaver. And, says Carroll, notice the black willow: "This can become one of the tallest willows, a clump with twisting branches," he says, "but along more active flood zones like these, it's more of a ground cover, sheared by water and ice and sand. Because the water shears them back, they don't develop into shrubs here, much less trees." The black willow is a strong sprouting species. Its shoots are called sallows, and they are important food for beavers, deer, and wood turtles.

For another group of plants, the river's sand and cobblebars create an opportunity. "The river brings a ribbon of light" to what otherwise would be shaded by forest canopy, Carroll explains, and vines seize the day. Virginia creeper, poison ivy, and fox grape, with clusters of light green, unripe fruit and grasping tendrils, drape along one side of the river, flowing outward over the cobbles. These swift-growing vines can root in a shallow pocket of nutrients, and then twist and creep towards sunlight even on bare stone and sand.

"People try to restrain rivers, but they are a very dynamic element, always shifting around," says Carroll. The creatures that live here, instead, adapt to this river's extremes and opportunities. On cobblebars like these, Carroll recalls in his book, he often finds wood turtles. One day he found an old male, perhaps half a century old, who had halted in midstep in his progress along a beaver trail through reeds and willow. His faceted carapace, wrote Carroll, "had been reworked to Inuit-carving smoothness—worn smooth as a river stone."

Lawn Grass

Alien Invader

⤜

"*A* child said, 'What is the grass?' fetching it to me with full hands," Walt Whitman wrote in his poem "Song of Myself."

"How could I answer the child? I do not know what it is any more than he."

The poet went on to guess that grass "must be the flag of my disposition, out of hopeful green stuff woven ... or I guess it is the handkerchief of the Lord, a scented gift and remembrancer designedly dropt ..."

Today's suburbanite might well think that Whitman must have had some lawn.

"People think grass *is* your lawn," laments Lisa Standley, an environmental engineering consultant who teaches courses on native grasses at the New England Wild Flower Society's Garden in the Woods. Nothing could be further from the truth. Lawn grass is about as poetic as astroturf. Wild, native grasses are the stuff of poetry.

Some grasses can grow sixty feet tall. They can dance and glisten, arch and spread. Their seedheads glow like candles in the sun, or cascade like waterfalls, or shoot skyward like fountains.

Grass has flowers, fruits, and leaves. A grass might have little hairs and spines, giving the plant a translucent quality in the afternoon sun. Grass provides nesting material, food, and cover for everything from rabbits to quail to dragonflies. And grass is astonishingly varied: there are more than ten thousand species of grass worldwide, three hundred of them in New England.

Ubiquitous, constant, and familiar, native grasses are so much a part of the natural landscape that we sometimes fail to notice them. "You have to tune your eye to detail," explains Standley. "It's about learning to see how different each one is. If you can appreciate beauty in diversity, you've got a foundation for developing ways of protecting the things that are important."

Look for native grasses in the woods, along unmowed parts of roadsides, in rocky or acid soils. These plants are often as tough as they are beautiful. Consider planting some in your garden. Among those to watch for:

- Little bluestem: (*Schizachyrium scoparium*) Look for its clumps of coppery leaves on acid, sandy, dry soils, often growing in association with asters.
- Pennsylvania sedge (*Carax pennsylvanicus*): You've almost certainly seen this slender, graceful, bright-green grass growing in big patches in the woods, growing among ferns and wildflowers. "People drool over this when it's planted in gardens," says prairie advocate Sara Stein.
- Northern dropseed (*Sporobolus heterolepsis*): Looks like a small fountain, with hair-fine leaves, airy seed heads, and a nutty, spicy fragrance. Deep rooted, it will grow equally well in wet or dry soil.
- Switchgrass (*Panicum virgatum*): A wonderful cover for wildlife, this tall grass grows in two-foot-diameter clumps. Its curling blades turn gold in autumn.
- Indian grass (*Sorghastrum nutans*): Growing up to seven feet tall, its large, feathery seed head turns a rich ochre in fall. This grass is typical of the eastern prairie that once covered much of New England.
- Purple lovegrass (*Eragostis spectabilis*): One of the most beautiful native grasses, purple lovegrass grows scattered along roadsides. In the summer, its clouds of tiny flower

clusters look like clouds of raspberry-colored vapor rolling along the ground.

"When I start opening their eyes to how many grasses there are out there," says Standley, "people are amazed." In a 200-foot walk along the road, she can point out twenty or thirty different types of grass. "People find it incredible that grass is so beautiful, so diverse."

No wonder folks who love grass hate lawns.

"Lawns are ridiculously expensive, ecologically arid, an area in which nothing can live but its own pests," says Stein, a pioneer of gardening with grasses and author of *Planting Noah's Garden*. A lawn, she says, is the ecological equivalent of asphalt.

"We tell our clients we don't do lawns and we don't do poison ivy," says Selinda Chiquoine, a great fan of ornamental grasses and co-owner of Flowers Anonymous plantscaping firm in Sharon, New Hampshire. In fact, she prefers poison ivy: "At least poison ivy is a nice, natural, deep green and healthy in summer." And at least poison ivy is native. Though the lawn practically defines the suburban American landscape, not a blade of it is native. The grass on your lawn, like the grass in your pasture, is almost certainly composed of foreign plants that have been forced to live an artificial, chemically dependent lifestyle.

It's even living under an assumed name. America's most popular lawn grass, Kentucky bluegrass, is neither. It's not from Kentucky—it's from England. It's not blue, either—and it's not even naturally green for long. In the summer, most of the lawns in America—and we're talking about 50,000 square miles here, an area larger than Pennsylvania—would be brown as toast if we didn't spend $30 billion a year and a third of eastern America's municipal water supply keeping it green.

"Basically, we're making bonsai grass, literally cutting it to within an inch of its life," says Sarah Shobrun of the New England Wild Flower Society.

Mowing, fertilizing, and watering keeps lawn grass from doing what it really wants to do: shoot up to two feet tall, produce seeds, and turn brown.

Actually, if your lawn could do what it really wanted, it

would go home to England, says Stein. "These grasses don't belong in our country," she says. "They don't know how to cope. They need sheep. They need cool. They need rainfall."

These were the conditions under which the few grass species that now make up most American lawns spent the last several millennia. English grass is turf grass, which means it generally spreads like a carpet and tolerates continuous grazing. Turf grass thrives in a cool, wet climate.

Our native American grasses literally grew up in another world. These species are called bunch grasses and spread by clumping. They, too, have adapted to grazers. (All grasses have bits of glass-like silica in them, to slow the grazers down. But grazers evolved high-crowned teeth and thick enamel to crunch through the silica.) But native American grasses are adapted to the gustatory attentions of migratory animals like buffalo: they come, they nosh, they leave. Native grasses grow most vigorously during the hottest time of the year, not the wettest. And our American grasses generally produce seed in the fall—conveniently for migrating birds and seed-storing rodents.

So what are the English turf grasses doing over here?

They first appeared in our pastures, after European settlers discovered that American grasses made inferior fodder for their livestock. Some pastures were intentionally planted with turf seed, others may have sprung up from the seeds in imported hay.

But lawns were another matter.

Lawns had been popular in England since Tudor times, but mainly on estates. Lawns did not come to America until after the Civil War, with publication of Frank J. Scott's *The Art of Beautifying Suburban Home Grounds* in 1870. "Let your lawn be your home's velvet robe," Scott exhorted. "A smooth, closely shaven surface of grass is by far the most essential element of beauty of the grounds of a suburban house."

By these words Scott, and his followers doomed a handful of sturdy English grasses to a lifetime of exile, and millions of suburban homeowners to summer Saturdays toiling behind a lawnmower.

It's a circuit few Americans have dared escape, however. For as Michael Pollan, an editor at *Harper's* magazine, writes in his book *Second Nature*, maintaining the suburban lawn is not about grass gardening. It is an act of "recopying the same green sentence over and over: 'I am a conscientious homeowner. I share your middle-class values.'"

But today, Pollan, Standley, and Stein are among the mavericks leading a revolt against the monotonous monoculture of the lawn. At her Westchester County home in New York, Stein doesn't have a lawn; she has an eastern prairie of wildflowers and bluestem, whose story is told in *Planting Noah's Garden*.

Much of Pollan's lawn has been converted to orchard and garden. He's hired a kid to mow what's left of it. And Standley, too, has replaced much of the turf with flowers, ornamental grasses, and ground covers. But she confesses she'll probably keep at least a remnant patch of lawn. It may be wasteful, it may be monoculture, but the lawn does have its use: "After all," she says, "how else can you play croquet?"

Wild Berries

*M*ore than 140 summers ago, a single pursuit dominated the thoughts of a leading New England
philosopher: picking wild berries.

Henry David Thoreau would gaze at Mount Monadnock
each summer and think of blueberries: "fresh, dewy, almost
crispy blueberries, just in prime." On August 4, 1860, he was so
eager to pick that he rose before sunrise to gather them from
Monadnock's slopes. To his surprise, he ran into crowds of other
men and women, who, like him, were rushing up the mountain
in the dark and wet to gather the wild harvest.

Ralph Waldo Emerson grew frustrated with his friend
Thoreau and criticized his lack of worldly ambition. "Instead of
being the head of American engineers," groused the transcen-
dentalist, "he is captain of a huckleberry party."

But during the summer, it's hard to imagine a better way to
spend your time.

Huckleberries and dewberries beckon from aging fields.
Mulberries fruit along city sidewalks. Wild cranberries fatten in
northern bogs. What makes for a really bumper crop?

A snowy winter, a rainy spring and a showery summer will
produce spectacular wild crops of berries, according to Tom
Wessels, director of the Environmental Biology Program at Anti-
och/New England Graduate School in Keene, New Hampshire.
Canoeing around ponds and lakes or hiking granite mountains

like Thoreau's beloved Monadnock, you'll see both high-bush and low-bush blueberries laden with fat, juicy fruit. Cycling country roads or hiking through overgrown fields or along abandoned logging roads, you'll see loads of blackberries, raspberries, and, on vines growing closer along the ground, dewberries. If you're an avid bird watcher, birds can help lead you to many berries.

"Get out," advises Massachusetts state botanist Paul Somers. "Take advantage of it!"

If you're new to foraging, some of our most abundant native berries make particularly safe and easy quarry: anything that looks like a blueberry is almost certainly a blueberry (unless it's an equally delicious huckleberry). And though not everything that resembles a raspberry really is a raspberry, it's a pretty sure bet it's something safe and delicious.

Blueberries and huckleberries grow on small-leafed bushes alongside ponds and lakes and on granite mountains, providing the perfect snacks for canoeists and hikers. Huckleberries are darker, shinier, and a bit seedier than blueberries. You'll often find both growing together, though huckleberries prefer slightly drier soils. Watch for these berries ripening into September. They may stay on the bushes into October, at which point their relatives, the cranberries, start ripening in bogs.

Relatives of roses, red raspberries, black raspberries, black-berries, and dewberries look similar and grow on prickly stems in "shaggy" areas like abandoned fields and old logging roads. Dewberries look like blackberries, but appear on low-growing creepers instead of upright canes. Along rural roads in southeastern Massachusetts, look for their orange-colored, Oriental relative. Early New England whalers who had visited China were so impressed by the tasty wineberries they found there that they brought some back to plant in Buzzard's Bay yards. Now they grow wild.

Elderberries are the fruit of the American elder, a shrubby tree whose creamy white blossoms transform into hundreds of tart blue or black berries by mid-August or so. The berries are so small and numerous that a good way to separate each from its stem is to pick with an Afro comb. Not overly sweet, they combine well with apples and gooseberries in pies, make fabulous wine and jam, and, like blueberries, freeze well without sweetening.

Mulberries are "the most common but most neglected berry in the city," says Russ Cohen, the Rivers Advocate for the Massachusetts Fish and Wildlife Department and a wild-foods enthusiast who often teaches at the New England Wild Flower Society's Garden in the Woods in Framingham. When he rides his bike in the city, he looks for purple stains on the sidewalks, knowing that by glancing up he'll find a mulberry tree.

If you've missed a favorite fruit's season in your area, don't dispair: drive north. Each fifty miles extends the season by another week.

People aren't the only ones enjoying the feast. Windham County forester William Guenther was looking forward to a particularly good harvest from the wild raspberries growing behind his house in Newfane, Vermont, one summer—but someone else got to them first. On his way out to pick a snack, Guenther woke up a well-fed bear who was sleeping off a meal in the driveway. The two-pound bear scat Guenther discovered at his doorstep left little doubt about where the berries had gone: it was loaded with raspberry seeds.

Berries are such important summer foods for bears that one Minnesota study estimates blueberries alone provide 80 percent of the black bear's August diet. Just a few years back, a drought-induced berry failure (followed by an equally disastrous acorn and beechnut crop) so upset southern New England's bears that hunger forced some of them out of woods into cornfields, dumps, and even back yards. (At least one western Massachusetts cook reported a pie set out to cool on the back porch fell prey to an ursine thief.)

But summer's abundance usually means there's enough for everyone. Even carnivores, including foxes, skunks, raccoons, and coyotes, love wild berries; Assumption College botany professor Judith Sumner once had a dog who used to patiently pluck raspberries and blackberries from roadside bushes.

All of this is fine with the berry plants. While most creatures are rather adamant in their efforts to avoid getting eaten—that's what the thorns on raspberries and blackberries are for—fruits are another story. "We think of berries in terms of eating them," says Wessels, "but for the plant, the fruit is a reproductive strategy."

Each individual raspberry, for example, is a mature ovary of the raspberry plant. Each tiny seed inside represents an individual fertilization from pollen brought by beetles, wasps, and bees. (Each seed can, in theory, claim a different father—just like every puppy in a litter.) Each seed can turn into a baby raspberry. But first, it needs the right place to grow.

Plants have evolved various strategies for disseminating their offspring. Milkweed's downy parachutes float seeds miles away; big, heavy seeds like acorns may be carried off and buried by squirrels, who stay fairly near the parent tree. Berry bushes adopt a strategy in between: they want their young to grow not too near the parent, but not too far away, either. A few hundred yards to a mile or so away would be just right. The sweet berries are merely a ploy to co-opt some animal into transporting the seeds.

For many summer berries, the perfect courier for the errand is a bird. That's why so many fruits are red, points out Sumner: like red flowers, red fruits attract color-conscious, sharp-eyed birds—most of whom, in summer, stick fairly close to the nest. They delightedly eat the fruit and, hours later, deposit the seed conveniently with its own packet of fertilizer—ensuring a new crop for the next generation.

Hitchhiking the Gulf Stream

ॐ

*T*he fishermen at Seaport Fish in Rye, New Hampshire were astonished. When a lobsterman emptied his pots that summer day, along with the usual crustacean quarry, out came a strange interloper: a six-inch fish with an electric-blue tint, a huge triangular head, a jaw shaped like a parrot's beak, and huge spines on its fins.

It resembled nothing you'd expect to find in New England waters; it looked like an exotic escapee from some tropical reef.

And that, in fact, was what it was.

At Odiorne Point State Park's Seacoast Science Center in Rye, where the fish proved to be a popular exhibit, program director Steve Miller identified the creature as a grey trigger-fish—a denizen of the warm waters of Florida, Georgia, and the Carolinas, hundreds of miles to the south.

The triggerfish, who grew to more than a foot long and was nicknamed Ben, created quite a sensation at the Science Center—in part because of his unnerving habit of raising the spines of his fins and locking them together to hold him in place among the rocks of his exhibit while he slept. "He's so tropical, and so different," said Miller, "and people are amazed you can find something like that here."

Normally, the southernmost end of the Gulf of Maine, Cape Cod, acts as a biological barrier to marine life, since its waters are usually 10° colder than the water south of the Cape, explained Miller. But, as Center Director, Wendy Lull, points out, "There are lots of different species being transported around that we're not aware of."

In fact, even in the Gulf of Maine's frigid waters, you might be swimming with an irridescent butterfly fish from Carribean reefs this summer. In Rhode Island bays, you could find yourself snorkeling with sea horses. And who knows? If you're a sport fisherman, you might find on the end of your hook a tropical gamefish like a jack or a grouper—or even a bright-crimson tropical bigeye, which a Rhode Island fisherman recently pulled out of Jamestown's waters.

Unbeknownst to most of us, tropical fish are hitchiking north along periodic eddies in the Gulf Stream. These eddies create temporary, natural warm-water highways—like rivers in the sea—bringing strange and beautiful aliens to New England shores.

Their odyssey is, as Steve Miller says, "an amazing fish tale." The story begins with the Gulf Stream. Born in warm tropical seas, the Gulf Stream flows north along the southeast coast of the U.S., sometimes as fast as one hundred miles a day, until it is pushed off-shore by underwater hills off the Carolinas. But about eight times a year, a confluence of wind, temperature, and salinity changes creates spiralling warm-water masses called eddies—and it's these huge masses of wayward waters that bring tropical fish north to our waters.

"These eddies are amazing," said Miller. "We're talking about water masses the size of the state of Massachusetts, spinning off loaded with plankton and seaweeds and animals."

The eddies can happen at any time of year, but in seasons other than summer, any hitchikers are usually quickly doomed. (Though not always: the fisherman who hooked that striking red bigeye pulled it out of 42° Jamestown waters in December.) New England waters are simply too cold most of the year for tropical fish to survive for long.

That's why summer affords your best chance to glimpse some of these tropical visitors up north. And that's also why the New England Aquarium collects these tropical travellers each year: this way they can conveniently augment their collection by rescuing vagrants who would otherwise be doomed to die.

Each September and often also in October, the Aquarium mounts a three- or four-diver collecting expedition to Ft. Wetherall in Jamestown and the bays and shallows of Newport. "The first time I went, I couldn't believe it," said aquarist Sally Rosen. "There were trunk fish everywhere, pipe fish—I was overwhelmed that I was diving in New England and seeing these things."

Trunk fish are also called boxfish for their strange appearance. Their bodies are encased in a rigid, box-like skin, with the eyes, mouth, and fins emerging through openings. Home aquarists seldom have luck with these unusual fish because if threatened they release a poison into the water, which kills everything in the tank, including the boxfish. The pipe fish, another Carribean species, is an eel-like creature whose snaky shape sometimes inspires sea horses to hitch a ride on them, holding on with their gripping tails.

Beachgoers watching the team collect colorful reef fish in their nets were dumbstruck. "They said they were going to bring their masks and snorkels next time!" Rosen said.

Most of the dozen or so specimens collected on each expedition are thumbnail-sized youngsters, she said. Caught up in the Gulf Stream, these juveniles travel north from the Caribbean along with sargasso weed, until they are swept into an eddy. Some of them are pretty battered and skinny after the long journey. They travel back to the Aquarium in super-oxgenated water to feast on delicacies like oysters and scallops in isolation tanks before they go on exhibit. About fifty tropical fish in the aquarium's collection were obtained from New England waters. You can see them in the 60-gallon Southern Visitors tank beside the Edge of the Sea display, and others in the Giant Ocean tank.

Ben the triggerfish was in bad shape, too, when he first came to the Seacost Science Center that August. He was not the first of Miller's triggerfish patients, though: another had been brought to him in 1993, but died of the cuts and bruises it had sustained on its long journey. Ben was luckier, and he lived to a ripe old age.

Unlike many aquarium fish, Ben was a keen observer of the world outside his tank, and when you walked into the room, "this fish not only noticed you, he seemed to be able to differentiate between familiar and unfamiliar people," Miller wrote in an article for New Hampshire Audubon. "He was really quite a showman," Lull agreed. "Everyone gravitated toward him."

Disappearing Bees

*M*any plants face what humans would consider an
embarrassing social problem. "Let's face it," says
pollination expert Stephen Buchmann, research entomologist at
the Carl Hayden Bee Research Center in Tucson, Arizona,
"plants can't get up and go on a date."

Enter the birds and, especially, the bees—sex brokers extra-
ordinaire. Lately, though, the bees are making that entrance by
an unlikely venue: they're coming by truck. In fact, the bees that
pollinated the flowers that turned into the cranberries you
bought for Thanksgiving last year probably came out of a semi
from North Carolina instead of a hive in some local hollow tree.

Each summer, scores of trucks swarm up the interstates from
points south. Under cover of darkness (because that's when the
bees are asleep), each truck brings hundreds of thousands of honeybees to pollinate New England's apple orchards and cranberry
bogs—because there aren't enough honeybees already there to do
the job.

By some estimates, New England beekeepers may have lost
50 to 70 percent of their honeybee population in just two years—
victims of the foreign varroa mite that threatens honeybees nationwide. For the "wild" honeybees that nest in hollow trees, the
picture's even worse. U.S. Department of Agriculture entomologists say most of them may already be dead.

But before you mourn the loss of another native species,

consider this: our "wild" honeybees are really just escapees from keepers' hives. Honeybees weren't native to America to begin with. Like the varroa mite, the honeybee was a foreign immigrant. (The most popular honeybees are Italian.)

Before honeybees arrived with European settlers 375 years ago, our native insects, bats, and birds accomplished the job of pollination quite nicely, thank you. Buchmann and desert ecologist Gary Paul Nabhan call them *The Forgotten Pollinators*, the title of a book and a public awareness campaign to protect pollinators, conserve rare plants, and draw attention to some of the little-known pollinators in our own back yards.

New England, for instance, hosts some five hundred species of native bees—yet most people can't name one of them besides the bumble. Yellowjackets? Wrong—they're not bees. Stinging does not make an insect a bee—eating pollen and nectar does. Yellowjackets, like other wasps and hornets, may eat an occasional pollen snack, but mostly they are carnivores, feasting on insects even less appreciated than themselves, such as flies.

Many of our native bees don't even look like bees. Some are green, blue, or red. Search the plumes of goldenrod, the crowns of thistle, and petals of the last mallows, and you'll see some bees are as small as fruit flies. Others, like the black carpenter bees who bore holes in wood, are twice the size of bumble bees.

Some of our native bees look just like honeybees, but act differently. Some fly only at night, pollinating evening primrose. The "unheralded heroes of the squash patch," as Buchmann calls them, are little honeybee-size and -color natives who do their best work at 4:30 in the morning. You've probably never seen one, but they deserve the credit for your pumpkins, squash, and cucumbers.

Most of our native bees, like all but 5 percent of the 25,000 bee species scientists have described world-wide, aren't social, colonial insects like hive-nesting honeybees. They're solitary creatures that nest singly in little holes in the ground. Rather than produce gallons of honey for a hive of 200,000, solitary female bees make a little ball of pollen and nectar and lay some eggs on it.

Because they don't have a huge hive to defend, solitary bees are generally gentle—some don't even have stingers. Honeybees are generally calm when they're pollinating flowers, but if you disturb the hive, they'll defend it fearlessly, en masse, on behalf of their hundred-thousand kin.

Honeybees' nasty, barbed stings give scientists who study native bees one more strike against the exotic interlopers usurping our natives' rightful pollen. ("We call the Italian bees 'pollen pigs,'" confesses Brian Danforth, a Cornell entomologist and self-described "solitary bee worker.") Bernd Heinrich, professor of Zoology at the University of Vermont, has calculated that each honeybee hive consumes the pollen resources of 102 bumblebee colonies.

American agriculture has become so vulnerably dependent on foreign honeybees that USDA entomologists warn if anything happens to the honeybees we could face a "pollination crisis" of disastrous proportions. As it is, California's almond acreage alone requires 800,000 beehives—about half of which need to be trucked into California from other states.

Since 1947, the number of America's managed honeybee colonies have plummeted from six million to fewer than two million. That's why entomologists worry about the varroa mite—the third and worst new bee disease to plague American beekeepers in the past twenty-five years.

The little red mites first appeared in the U.S. in 1987, hitchhiking on infected bees from Paraguay (which had themselves caught the mite from bees that had been shipped legally to Paraguay as a present from Japan). The mites and their pupae suck blood from both pupal and adult honeybees. They're particularly damaging to developing pupae. Those that survive infestation become deformed, malnourished adults—and can spread the mites to "clean" colonies easily, since drones often visit neighboring hives. "Eliminating or controlling the varroa mite is one of the most challenging problems to confront the bee industry," says Justin Schmidt, an entomologist with the USDA and a member of the Entomological Society of America.

"It's having a profound effect," says New Hampshire Fish

and Game animal damage control agent Rob Calvert. "It's taken the hobby beekeepers just about out of the picture. Some bee-keepers are going back to school for computer technology jobs."

Northern honeybees are particularly hard-hit, explains Calvert, whose own hives have dropped from twenty a few years ago to nine today. Harsh winters always kill a certain portion of New England's overwintering honeybees; the varroa mite weakens stressed bees further. (Northern beekeepers replace new bees each spring from southern sources, where bees can breed year-round. The new bees usually arrive in three-pound packages sent through the mail—and "boy, the post office is quick to call you that morning when your bees have arrived!" says Calvert. "It's almost a wake-up call.")

"When the apple blossoms were in bloom, people were desperate to get the bees in there working the fruit," said Artie Favreau, who, with his wife Deb ("the Queen Bee" around here, he says), keeps 125 hives in Sterling, Massachusetts. Migrant and local beekeepers answered the call, he said, and the apple harvest was assured.

As the varroa mite hit, beekeepers were still struggling to cope with a different mite, known as the tracheal mite, which hit the U.S. back in 1984. According to Roger Morse, Professor of Beekeeping at Cornell University in Ithaca, New York, this pest arrived on Africanized bees smuggled to America from Brazil. (Why would anyone intentionally import aggressive Africanized bees? Because even though they are dangerous, explains Morse, they are better honey producers than the gentler European honeybees.)

Before the tracheal mite, a fungal disease called chalkbrood nearly eradicated the German race of European honeybees in America. (The fungus got here on legally imported bee pollen—before people realized that pollen could host bee diseases.) No treatment was ever found for that disease.

Fortunately, the varroa mite can be treated (though not entirely cured) by hanging a "No-Pest-Strip" mite-killer in the hive. As researchers search for a cure, Buchmann and Nabhan suggest the non-beekeeping public can help avert the pollination crisis by giving our native solitary bees a boost. Consider erecting a beehouse: a few holes drilled in scrap lumber and mounted under your eaves or some paper "sweetheart" straws glued to a milk carton left in a branch will attract native bees to nest near your home.

Sound unlikely to catch on? That's what skeptics said about bat houses.

"About every third bite of food we take, we owe to pollinators like bees," Buchmann reminds us. "We owe them a break."

Plants' Healing Poisons

⅗

*W*hen herbalist Deb Soule goes walking in spring meadows and woods, she sees healing everywhere. In the common mullein's leaves and flowers, she sees a cough syrup; in rhododendron, a cure for toothache; among the hawthorn trees, a heart tonic. From herbs and flowers, trees and lichens, she makes the teas and tinctures, balms and oils she sells at Avena Botanicals, her herbal apothecary in Rockport, Maine. "All the medicine we need," she asserts, "is growing right around us."

But when Judith Sumner, who teaches botany at Assumption College in Worcester, Massachusetts, walks the woods, she sees, instead, an ancient struggle. She sees mullein trying to choke caterpillars, rhododendrons staking out territory, and hawthorns repelling the assaults of moose, deer, and rabbits.

Soule sees plants' powers to help humankind; Sumner sees their talents for poisoning their enemies.

Even though they are rooted to one spot, plants defend themselves, stake out territories, lure certain creatures to pollinate them, and repel others. "Plants may seem inanimate, but they're not at all!" Sumner said as she walked through the New England Wild Flower Society's Garden in the Woods in Framingham, Massachusetts. The low, showy white flowers of the bloodroot in front of her seemed innocent as snow, but Sumner knows better. "They don't pounce and claw at you," she said, "but they can get you."

Plants invented chemical warfare, and they've been perfecting their weapons for 135 million years. First in the arsenal were the ethereal oils, produced in special cells in the earliest flowering plants, the magnolias and their relatives. Beetles, who began to evolve about the same time the first flowering plants hit the scene, don't like the taste. But we do: these chemicals give Carolina allspice, bay laurel, and cinnamon their special flavor and scent.

Later plants developed other compounds to ward off new predators. Hollyhocks produce chemicals to clog insects' mouth parts; mulliens accomplish the same with wooly hairs on the stem and leaves. Rhododendrons produce a chemical that makes it impossible for other plant species to grow near its roots.

As caterpillars, birds, and mammals appeared, plants evolved new strategies. Bitter-tasting alkaloids—including caffeine, cocaine, and nicotine—attacked the mammalian nervous system. Glycosides affected the heart muscles.

Bloodroot's secret weapon is the alkaloid, sanguinarine. Nibble the blood-red root, and you could get tunnel vision; chewing a handful of leaves could leave you vomiting for hours.

But gathered carefully, prepared knowledgeably and taken in the right dosage, bloodroot can remove warts, ease pain, stimulate the appetite, and fight infection. Native Americans used the root as an ingredient in cough medicine and in tea for rheumatism, asthma, bronchitis, and fevers.

"Many medicinal plants are well-known poisons," says Sumner. "Dose, time of year, and the part ingested all influence whether a plant is toxic or medicinal."

Native American herbalists knew this well; they knew that carefully used minute amounts of toxic sheep laurel's pink and white flowers could ease bowel ailments and how to harvest and prepare the bitter leaves for backache, cold, and stomach pain. They knew how to make teas to ease cramps from the root of the red baneberry, and teas to treat kidney and bladder infections from the leaves of the mayflower. Other plants provided balms and poultices: slit the succulent stems of jewelweed and rub on the sticky sap, and the poison ivy you just walked through won't give you a rash.

American colonists were quick to borrow from their hosts' apothecaries. Daniel Boone made more money selling American ginseng (which is now endangered due to overcollecting) than he did from trapping and selling furs; the root was considered an excellent tonic. Lydia Pinkham of Lynn, Massachusetts made her family rich selling Pinkham's Vegetable Compound, a tincture of four herbs macerated in alcohol, which promised to restore health and beauty to women of the late 19th century. The ingredients—unicorn root, black cohosh, golden ragwort, and butterfly weed—were well-known to native Americans.

American immigrants, too, had a rich tradition of using healing plants, and brought many of their own to American soils. In fact, many common plants we consider typically American—from the day lily to the yellow-flowering roadside lesser celandine poppy to the stalked purple blooms of foxglove—are actually foreign medicinal plants which escaped colonists' gardens. Gypsies brought day lilies from India across Eastern Europe to America and prized them as cathartics, blood cleaners, and tonics. The European lesser celandine's caustic juice was used as a wart remover. Foxglove, with thirty different glycosides, was used as a remedy for dropsy, and provides one of the most important heart drugs in modern medicine today, digitalis.

Still, for centuries, Western medicine lagged behind older cultures in herbal knowledge. The ancient Egyptians used blue-green molds as antibiotics; the sacred Hindu "Vedas" described a cure for leprosy 1500 years ago; and the Chinese used plants to treat asthma thousands of years before the American discovery of the identical chemical, ephedrine, in the 1920s.

But American medicine may be catching up with this ancient knowledge. Since Soule founded her herbal business more than a decade ago she's witnessed "a tremendous re-awakening of interest in herbs." She's often asked to speak at conferences before family physicians, because so many of their patients are—with or without a doctor's advice or consent—using healing herbs bought at health food stores. Drug companies, too, are interested in many of the plants you'll see emerging in your nearest woodland: hellebore's deeply ribbed leaves posses an alkaloid, veratrine, which lowers blood pressure. The spring May apple has a substance that prevents cell division and may be useful in cancer therapy. And extracts from bloodroot are now added to commercial mouthwash and toothpaste to help fight plaque.

In her book *Enduring Harvests*, ethnobotanist E. Barrie Kavash gives recipes for many of the foods and remedies made from native plants; Deb Soule's *The Roots of Healing* concentrates on herbal tonics and remedies for women. "The plants beneath our feet have powers and potentials that could make you see them in a whole different way," says Kavash, who is part Creek, Cherokee, and Powhatan Indian. "Plants are our educators and indicators. They have a lot to communicate."

The World
Between Sand Grains

⑥

*S*un-bathers lie atop a carpet of jewels. Children build castles from ancient mountains. Beneath the beachcomber's feet, miniature worlds seethe and swirl in a frenzy of hunting and hiding, traveling, and feeding.

The world of beach sand is a place of astonishing wonders, where each grain of sand can claim a rich history, and a stretch of "barren" beach can support millions of hidden lives. Beach sand is so rich, in fact, that a whole specialized cosmos of creatures are even adapted to living and moving in the spaces between individual sand grains.

"The sandy beach is far from a desert," says Wendy Lull, director of the Seacoast Science Center at Odiorne State Park in Rye, New Hampshire. "There's a lot going on, but you need to hone your observational skills to see it. There's a lot to see if you know how to look."

That's not always an easy task. "In the sands, almost all is hidden," the great conservationist and marine biologist Rachel Carson observed. The creatures who live in beach sand are masters of camouflage and concealment. Tiger beetles, sand fleas, and mole crabs hide in sandy burrows; moon snails hunt up to a foot beneath wet sand. Piping plovers' sand-colored eggs and plumage are so perfectly matched to their surroundings that most people never realize these birds nest on bare sand on some of Massachusetts' busiest beaches—hidden in plain sight.

Even sand itself hides its true identity: a stretch of beach may look like a vast expanse of sameness, yet it is actually, of course, a huge collection of individual grains, each one as distinctive as a snowflake or fingerprint. "It is not an exaggeration to say that each grain has its own unique story to tell," writes physicist James S. Trefil in his book, *A Scientist at the Seashore*.

"Sand grains are old mountains that have been re-distributed," explains New England Aquarium biologist and broadcaster Paul Erickson. Sand is mostly weathered rock—minerals pulverized by the process of the uplift that forms mountains, rocks washed downstream by rivers and brooks.

Scientists study the origins and history of sand grains to learn about the geological structure of the lands that once lay upstream. Streaks of black magnetite on Plum Island beaches, for instance, originated in the White Mountains of Maine and New Hampshire. Most of New England's sands record the debris deposited by retreating Ice Age glaciers: colorless quartz punctuated by amber feldspar and black igneous rock.

Even a casual observer can tell a thing or two about the history of a sand grain. Rounded sand grains have been polished by wind. Rougher grains were brought by water. Most sand is quartz, the most abundant mineral on earth. But a small sample of sand could contain a dozen different minerals, from blue, glass-like grains of cyanite to the dark green of glauconite, a form of iron. New England's sands often sparkle with jewels: Pink and red grains are pure garnets; purple ones, amethyst. Forget legends of streets paved with gold; you can spread your beach blanket on a carpet of ground gems.

While New England beaches are derived almost entirely from rock, warmer beaches may be composed in part—sometimes almost entirely—of fragments of tiny sea creatures: crushed corals, pieces of shell, a rubble of skeletons from plants and animals. On U.S. beaches south of Virginia, about 5 percent of beach sand is composed of calcareous or shell sand. Silver Sands Beach, Grand Bahama, is composed almost exclusively of coral skeletons. A significant portion of many South Pacific beaches are composed of dead sea lillies, actually animals whose remains yield distinctive, disk-shaped grains.

Atop, around, beneath the sand—even between each grain—life abounds. In the wet sand beneath your feet, the miniature neighborhood of individual sand grains is populated by tiny creatures collectively known as "interstitial fauna." This diverse group includes the world's smallest mollusks; worms only one-sixteenth of an inch long; tiny crustaceans; and weird creatures known as water bears, with eight clawed legs and a relatively large brain (considering the biggest water bear grows to only one millimeter in length), but no heart or respiratory system.

"These are some of the most obscure and exotic critters," says Dr. Eugene Gallagher, a biological oceanographer at the University of Massachusetts in Boston, "all extremely specialized for this strange life of moving between sand grains."

To them, explains Gallagher, "the sand grains are like giant, stacked cannonballs on a New England town square"—the spaces between grains seem copious. To move between them, most of these creatures wiggle like snakes or propel themselves with beating hairs called cilia. The water bears creep around using their claws. Many interstitial animals also posses an array of sensors to tell them which way is up (a mini version of our inner ear), whether it's dark enough (sunlight is usually bad news) and if they're comfortably ensconced between grains or not. And they also have special organs to attach themselves to individual grains, so they aren't washed away each time a wave comes by.

Interstitial animals feed on even tinier organisms brought to them with the tides—each wave, to them, is like a pizza delivery. And that's the case for many beach creatures: the sand offers shelter while the ocean brings food. Burrowers like marine worms feed passively beneath the waves, washing scraps of passing nutrients through their bodies. Mole crabs hunt at the edge of the water, moving in and out of the tide, eager to scavenge whatever the waves bring in. (Stand where the waves move over your feet, advises Lull, and look through the water at the sand below: sometimes you'll see a whole meadow of crab antenna waving at you.) In the litter of the tide line, beach fleas emerge to gnaw on dead fish or crabs. Sandpipers called sanderlings run in and out of the tide, eating the sand fleas.

It all balances rather neatly—until people and their vehicles blunder through. Though an individual grain of sand is almost indestructible, a beach is amazingly fragile. As Scott Hecker, who directs Massachusetts Audubon's Coastal Water Bird Program at Marshfield, points out, a single dune buggy driving over the wrong spot is sufficient to set off unnatural erosion, crush hundreds of least tern nests, or kill the under-sand roots of American beach grass (which can be found five feet away from the nearest visible plant). Sun-tanners, oblivious to sand-colored birds, position beach towels where plovers need to nest; unwitting beachcombers stroll where sanderlings need to feed. As a result, sanderling populations, by some estimates, have decreased by as much as 80 percent over the past thirty years.

Unless we can learn to tread more lightly, Hecker warns, the living sandy beach could become a desolate desert after all.

Letting the Coyote Stay Wild

❦

*I*n all his years working outdoors, Massachusetts state wildlife biologist Bill Davis had never caught more than a glimpse of a coyote flashing across the road. But one summer day, when he was working at Quabbin Reservoir, he spotted a family of nine—five puppies, two juveniles, and the parents—feeding on a deer carcass. With his binoculars, he watched them play and feast until dark. "It was a wonderful experience," he said, "words don't do it justice." But one thing that stays with him: even though he was a quarter mile from the family, when the adults saw him, they moved their pups even farther away.

Such wariness is typical of coyotes, say biologists. Could this be the same species that attacked three-year-old Daniel Neal while he was playing on his swingset in a Cape Cod back yard?

Experts on coyotes agree this incident was extremely abnormal—the only documented instance of a coyote attacking a person on the east coast. Though no one knows for sure, many suspect the errant coyote, a 43-pound male that police shot after the attack, was a formerly captive animal that a person had cared for when it was injured (an autopsy showed a healed fracture of the right front leg) or adopted as a pet and then unwisely released.

For weeks after the strange, upsetting incident, Susan Langlois' phone at the Massachusetts Division of Fisheries and Wildlife was ringing off the hook. "It's all I've been dealing with," she said at the time. People want to know why the attack happened. "But it's not like you're going to come out with a crystal-clear, 'Oh! That's why.'" As University of Massachusetts biologist Todd Fuller points out, animals, like people are individuals; possibly, the Sandwich coyote "was simply psychotic."

Two things, however, are virtually certain: first, this is not the behavior of a normal, wild coyote. Coyotes normally avoid people, spending their late summer days pouncing on grasshoppers, snacking on wild berries, and teaching their pups to hunt mice, frogs, and snakes.

But equally certain is a second fact: when people subvert the natural behavior of wild animals—tossing them food, enticing them with garbage, or adopting them as pets—they're asking for trouble, for both our species and theirs. In California, where homes sprawl into desert and where some people have enticed coyotes to their houses with food for decades, coyotes have injured twenty-one people in the past ten years.

"I think it's really a tragedy that coyotes and human beings are having trouble coexisting," says Hope Ryden, author of the landmark book *God's Dog: The North American Coyote*. "There has to be an effort on our side to make room for this animal without destroying its wildness."

On Cape Cod, there's ample evidence some people failed to respect that wildness. In 1992, a male coyote who'd been hit by a car was treated for a broken pelvis by a Falmouth veterinarian. While recuperating, the coyote was virtually immersed in the human world: the public visited him regularly. He was fed dead livestock (chicken and ground beef). He was given daily baths—an event most dogs would consider traumatic—and kept in a room where a stereo played heavy-metal rock music. He was later transferred to a wildlife rehabilitator, but escaped from his pen, and his whereabouts are unknown.

People are obviously feeding coyotes, on the Cape as well as elsewhere. One of Langlois' many callers reported that he had tossed a rock at a coyote, which the coyote sniffed. Was the animal trying to pick up his scent and track him down, the caller worried? Not at all. The coyote smelled the rock to see if it was, like other objects people had tossed his way, food.

People unwittingly provide coyotes with other unnatural handouts, too: by leaving cats, pet food, and unsecured garbage out at night, they are enticing coyotes into their yards.

Wildlife experts agree the threat of wild coyotes attacking more toddlers is virtually nil.

Coyotes are normally remarkably unaggressive. Hope Ryden once watched an elk calf prevent eight hungry coyotes from scavenging the carcass of another elk. Though the baby elk guarded its sibling's body for three days, it was never attacked.

"Pick up the newspaper on any day and you'll find plenty of other things to worry about," says Eric Orff, wildlife biologist with New Hampshire's Fish and Game Department. If you're worried for your children, Orff suggests, "I'd cast my eyes towards my human neighbors." In fact, your neighbor's child is more likely to bite your tot than any coyote is: daycare centers report this is surprisingly common. Your neighbor's dog is an even more likely suspect: half of all children are bitten by a dog at some point in their lives.

Still, as a parent, Orff understands the alarm. One day, years ago, when Orff's three-year-old was, like Daniel Neal, playing on the back yard swingset, his son was attacked by a wild animal—not a coyote, but a pheasant. It was an injured bird Orff himself had nursed and fed all winter and then released.

"These are anomalies," said Orff. "Now there are exactly the same number of attack pheasants and attack coyotes."

But alarm can spread quickly when it comes to predators, especially when the predator in question is an animal new to the area.

Coyotes had never been seen in the northeastern U.S. before the 1940s. When the animal was first spotted, no one knew what it was: a cross between coyotes and dogs? Small wolves? Genetic studies show the Eastern coyote is actually a hybrid, whose recent ancestors were gray wolves from southeastern Ontario and Quebec and western coyotes from Michigan, Ontario, and Minnesota.

Coyotes began to colonize the Northeast just as many of the native species—from bears to beavers—were returning after centuries of clear cutting and bounty hunting. But the coyotes' spread has been astonishingly swift: in New Hampshire, for instance, they swept from Colbrook to Seabrook in eight years—a territory it took bears half a century to regain.

Their spread attests to an extraordinary intelligence, resourcefulness, and adaptability. Coyotes can live anywhere from forests to the edge of cities. They can eat anything from grasshoppers to garbage (a New Hampshire study of coyote stomachs collected in the fall found they were eating more vegetation than meat). Their living arrangements are flexible: they can form packs like wolves, or live in small family units; often siblings from a previous litter help parents care for new pups, but if the pups are weaned, the father alone will care for a litter if the mother is killed.

In *God's Dog*, Ryden calls coyotes "Superdogs," for they possess senses and sensitivities even keener than man's best friend—and none of the domestic docility. Like dogs, coyotes are playful and affectionate; they are so fiercely loyal they will bring food to injured or trapped companions. (And they are jealous of their loved ones: In her book, Ryden describes a captive female so jealous of the mate she wanted that whenever he would pay attention to another female, she would knock him over and stand on him.)

And, like dogs, coyotes learn fast, as writer and naturalist Elizabeth Marshall Thomas (author of the bestselling *The Hidden Life of Dogs*) has observed. In her Peterborough, New Hampshire field, the coyotes quickly understood that mowing machines chop up tasty snakes and frogs, and reveal the runways of mice and voles. They actually follow the machine, at a distance of thirty feet, to maximize the hunting opportunities—much to the delight of Thomas, who enjoys watching them curl their feet up under the chest and spring, joyous and fox-like, to pin their prey.

But coyotes' ability to learn makes them uniquely vulnerable to the dangerous lessons people unwittingly teach. Researching her book, Ryden met a coyote in Yellowstone National Park, who, enticed by tidbits thrown from cars, patrolled the roads. The animal stood on her hind legs and placed her forefeet on the driver's open window. Ryden leapt out of her car to photograph the interaction, and watched in horror as a child reached out to pet the coyote. The animal snapped, but didn't bite. When Ryden got back to her vehicle, the coyote had leapt inside her car. (She got it out, ironically, by doing what she advises against: tossing it a peanut butter sandwich.) This coyote was later shot, after biting a child.

Wild coyotes' many talents won them the admiration of the western Indian tribes who shared their range. The Aztecs deified them. Crow Indian mythology holds the coyote was the First Worker, creator of the earth and its creatures and the founder of human customs.

But on the California set of "Dr. Quinn, Medicine Woman," near the site where University of Massachusetts biologist Fuller and his students study coyotes and bobcats, actress Jane Seymour says she hates coyotes. She has house cats, and coyotes consider them prey. (Much like house cats hunt chipmunks and birds, Orff points out: "Tit for tat.") House cats tend to disappear most often in June, when coyotes are weaning their pups.

Coyotes will also hunt small dogs, especially at night. So bring your pets in at night. Bring in their food, too. Secure your garbage.

If you would like to observe these fascinating animals, don't draw them to your home; watch them behaving naturally. Go to the edge of a newly mown field, especially around dusk, and you might see them pouncing on grasshoppers or hunting mice. Listen for their songs at night. (The best arias occur in February, when they sing love songs to their mates.)

"The coyote has a real function in the whole intricate web of wildlife that is crucial," Ryden says. "It's had to take the place of other predators we've exterminated—like wolves and mountain lions. This is not a domestic animal, but an animal performing an important role in nature."

That is, if we let it stay wild.

The Habitat of the Water Lily

ॐ

*I*f there is one time and place on Earth where you can believe, for a moment, that time stands still, it is on a pond
blanketed with water lilies in late August.

The lily pads lie flat and still as reflections on the water. The
fragrance of the sweet water lily's new blooms lingers long and
heavy, as we wish summer might. The blossoms themselves seem
to promise peace; the first position in hatha-yoga's path to medi-
tation is named for the lotus.

Lily pads invite repose. Look closely at the still life covering
the water. Among the bowl-shaped or notched pads you may
discover the black, thumb-shaped heads of painted and spotted
turtles, or the yellow-eyed bullfrog. The broad, flat leaves provide landing pads for dragonflies and damselfies, beetles, flies,
and bees.

But there's much more going on here. In Hindu mythology,
the timeless water lily symbolizes the opening to the womb of the
universe. Indeed, the water lily creates a universe of its own, and
much of it lies between and beneath its floating leaves and fragrant flowers.

"If you look carefully, you will find an entire population of
organisms gathered around the water lily—a little ecosystem,"
says Willam Niering, a botanist and wetlands ecologist at Connecticut College in New London.

Water lilies are certainly important to the life of the pond as a whole. In summer, beavers and muskrats eat the buds and pads; the beavers roll the leaves into double scrolls, clasping one roll in each fist before popping them into their mouths. In winter, they may subsist almost entirely on the lilies' thick starchy rhizomes, which they mine from pond-bottom muck.

A water lily, though, is more than just a food pantry for animals. This is not just a plant, but a place. In the spiked flowers of pickerel weed, the white blossomed arrowheads, and the standing armies of cattails—at the depth where you would step into a canoe, the plants form a miniature ecosystem, in their way as unique and as whole as a beech forest or an alpine meadow.

Michael Canduto, a teacher at the Vermont Institute of Natural Science, calls lily pads "microhabitats." The leaves dampen wave action and create calmer water, enabling the growth of the world's smallest flowering plants, (smaller than the head of a dressmaker's pin) floating duckweeds. The forest of underwater lily-flower stalks and leaf stems provides hatcheries for the eggs of snails and water insects, mites and beetles, and nurseries for bullheads, minnows, and sunfish.

Freshwater sponges float in these spaces, many of them colored a bright green with symbiotic algae. (You may notice a small sphere embedded within them in late summer. These are known as gemmules, the tough "winter buds" that allow the sponge to survive the winter.) The stems and undersides of lily leaves are coated with life. Some creatures spend all of their lives on, under, or within the nourishing tissues of the water lily.

Pluck a pad from the water and turn it over. The color may surprise you. The flip side of the rich green, leathery pad of the sweet water lily, for instance, is often crimson and hairy. You may find nothing—or you may come face-to-face with a large population of varied creatures.

"You can pick up ten leaves and not find anything," says Paul Fell, a professor of invertebrate zoology at Connecticut College. "Move on and look at another leaf, or in another place. Don't give up. You will find a wealth of things if you just keep on looking."

Ann Haven Morgan's classic *Field Book of Ponds and Streams* includes a diagram of fourteen animals found on the undersides of a single lily pad—and these are only those that are visible to the naked eye. Some of them you will recognize at once: several kinds of snails; bright-red water mites, relatives of the spiders; the arrow-headed flatworms known as planaria, which you may have had to cut up in high-school biology to watch them re-grow their severed parts.

Other inhabitants are more mysterious, such as the "moss animals" known as bryozoans—little creatures living in furry-looking colonies. Each strand of "fur" is really a tentacle-wreathed head, whirling around in the water, beating hair-like cilia to scoop particles of food into the animal's mouth. One species, which Fell has found especially abundant, is called Pectinatella; embedded in a gelatinous mass, it grows to the size of a softball.

Especially on the undersides of narrowly notched leaves of the yellow-flowered bullhead lily, you may find an odd construction that looks like a tiny leaf sandwich. This is the creation of the lily leaf caterpillar—one of the few caterpillars to live beneath the water, breathing through gills. The creature bites off two small pieces of leaf, arranges them shiny side-out, and fastens the edges together with strands of silk. The caterpillar itself forms the filling of the sandwich, which it then eats from the inside out.

The first gray and white adult moths emerge from these cases in June and July; a second generation produces caterpillars that sink down through the water in autumn and hibernate among the dying, frost-burned lily leaves.

On the undersides of lily pads, you're also likely to find a multitude of eggs. Whose are they? Tiny oval white eggs, glued separately to the underside of the leaf, belong to the whirligig beetle, the ubiquitous, flattened, oval creatures that congregate to walk and swim on the surface of still waters, circling round and round each other. Hatching ten days after the eggs are laid, the pale, worm-like beetle larva swim and prowl the pond bottom. Then one day, the larva will climb the lily stalk and hang upside down, and build a half-inch case around itself out of mud and saliva. Inside the case, it curls into a C-shape and pupates, hatching out as a beetle.

Small, oval, white eggs you might see arranged in curving rows around a small hole belong to the long-horned leaf beetle of the genus *Donacia*. You'll often see the metallic green or bronze adults walking along the tops of lily pads, touching the surface carefully with arched antennae. In late summer or early fall, the female bites a hole a quarter-inch in diameter through a pad, inserts her abdomen and deposits her eggs on the underside of the pad.

Her offspring hatch underwater, yet breathe air, for the water lily supplies the larvae with both an air hose and an oxygen tank. Each newly hatched larvae crawls down the stem of the lily, burrows into the mud, and bores a hole into the underground stem. With its head inside the air spaces of the stem, it taps the plant's air supply—and is surrounded by escaping air, even four or five feet below water. (The flood of bubbles you see breaking the surface is sometimes created by one of these babies.)

When a larva matures, it spins a waterproof, underwater cocoon; its air supply still provided by the plant. And when the adult beetle hatches out, it carries with it a little air tank as it rises to the surface. Hairs on the beetle's belly catch air bubbles from the leaking "hose" of the stem, a tiny balloon it rides to the surface. When it reaches a lily pad, it crawls atop it, and begins the cycle anew.

The Startling Beauty
of Underwing Moths

૩ৡ৹

*T*he bride may be at your window. The penitent might be on the porch. The darling awaits you in your back yard, perhaps keeping company with the old maid, the once-married, the relict, or the inconsolable.

If you've never noticed them, that's probably because they hide during the day, almost perfectly invisible. But each July and August, when they emerge from the dull-brown pupae hidden between leaves, the night comes alive with creatures whose sometimes doleful, sometimes romantic names hint at their mystery and intrigue: the *Catocala*, or underwing moths.

As their evocative common names suggest, these moths inspired great passions among the late 19th-century naturalists who named them, and even ignited feuds. "Moths are not the dull creatures some people think them to be," asserted Dave Winter, a dedicated moth-watcher in Westwood, Massachusetts, "They are greatly underrated, and that's a shame."

Moths are creatures of startling beauty and unexpected complexity—and no genus better illustrates this than the underwings. With wingspans sometimes more than three inches, they are some of the largest, as well as some of the most beautiful moths in North America—and yet you could easily mistake one for a piece of tree bark.

That's because the forewings of these moths are cryptically colored in drab grays and browns. Only when it parts its forewings does the creature reveal its breathtaking beauty: on the jet-black hindwings, some species sport crimson bands and white fringe, others have yellow bands, vibrant pink, or dramatic black and white.

If the sight of their brilliant underwings leaves you slack-jawed with astonishment, well, that's the idea: as the under-wings' startlingly beautiful hindwings evolved, they literally leave their predators' mouths agape.

In six decades of observing underwings and other moths, Winter, a retired pediatrician, often saw hungry birds, especially blue jays, attack these tasty insects. "But I've never seen a bird catch one," he said, "and my reaction is hooray!"

At the University of Massachusetts at Amherst, biology professor Theodore Sargent and his students have documented the moths' ingenious escape tactics in detail, releasing captured underwings to captive blue jays. Some jays, raised on mealworms, didn't know what to make of the moths. Because of their cryptic forewings, underwings are tough to spot at rest. Not only do they choose bark to match their color, but they also align themselves to take best advantage of the ridges and shadows of the surface. The dejected underwing, for instance, rests head down on hickory, while the relict underwing rests head up on white birch. (They practice this trick as caterpillars, feeding at night and staying motionless and nearly invisible by day.)

But even some birds who manage to get the insects in their beaks came away hungry, because of what the moth does next: when grabbed on one side of a wing, the moth flashes its startlingly colorful hindwing at the predator. "Almost like a human, the bird's jaw drops," Sargent said. "They're mystified as to what happened!"

Most underwing moths sport hindwing colors in variants of red and black or yellow and black, "biological warning signals, used with validity, by hornets, for example," as Winter wrote in a chapter of *Butterfly Gardening* published by the Xerxes Society and the Smithsonian Institution. No wonder, he observed, that our roadways' "stop" and "caution" signs, too, are so colored.

Underwings' strategy has proved extraordinarily successful: more than 200 species live worldwide, 106 of them in North America. So many species offered fertile ground for the nineteenth-century American naturalists who rushed to study and name them. As Sargent points out in his wonderful book on underwings, *Legion of Night*, because the ancients believed moths to be the souls of the dead, many of the earliest species described were given ghostly names in Latin, translating to the common names like the mourning underwing, the tearful underwing, the inconsolable. Next, naturalists turned to names evoking romantic tragedy: the bride, the consort, the sweetheart. Another suite of species are named after women famous for their lusts or talents: Delilah and Cleopatra, heroines from Shakespeare, Greek goddesses.

Nearly all the older *Catocala* names are female—probably because the people who named them were men. And, after all, they were spending a lot of time in the dark without female companionship. The underwings, however, do possess characteristics these men may have admired in the opposite sex: they are graceful and delicate, and the very name of the genus, *Catocala*, literally means "beautiful behind." And no wonder many were named after lusty women: these moths spend between two and thirteen hours engaged in the copulatory act (though not in a position many humans would care to attempt: tail tips joined and heads pointed in opposite directions, forming a diamond shape).

Like bar-room brawls over women, feuds over the newly described moths erupted regularly in the scientific journals of the day. As Sargent describes in his book, when Reverend George D. Hulst suggested in 1880 that some scientists were overeager to proclaim new species, English-born lepidopterist Augustus Grote sniped in reply, "Mr. Hulst likens the present knowledge of the species of *Catocala* to a diseased infancy. In this Mr. Hulst confounds the state of his own mind on the subject with that of others."

And when Pennsylvannia entomologist Herman Strecker sided with Hulst, Grote called Strecker's work "slovenly" and "inexcusable." "In vulgarity and misrepresentation," Grote wrote of his colleague, "he is, fortunately, without a rival." Strecker responded with equal valor: the Englishman had proposed naming a species after his own wife, but that, Strecker wrote, was a break in tradition: underwings were usually named after women of talent, he wrote.

Twentieth-century naturalists still get downright passionate about underwings. "Oho! my beauty!" chortled W.J. Holland, the Pittsburgh-based lepidopterist, in an account of a night of moth collecting in his 1905 *The Moth Book*: "Just above the moistened patch upon the bark is a great *Catocala*. The gray upper wings are spread, revealing the lower wings gloriously banded with black and crimson. In the yellow light of the lantern the wings appear even more brilliant than they do in sunlight. How the eyes glow like spots of fire!"

To attract these nectar- and sap-loving moths, Holland, like *Catocala* admirers today, painted patches of tree trunks with solutions of sugar and beer—a practice known as sugaring. Though simple concoctions work fine for the back yard naturalist, among avid moth-watchers, each champions a favorite brew: "And what kind of sugar must you use?" P. B. Allan asks rhetorically in a 1938 article. "Brown Barbados, my boy," he insists. "Eschew every other kind as the root of all evil where sugaring is concerned ... pay no heed to what your grocer tells you: clap a killing-bottle to his head and bid him stand and deliver Brown Barbados in abundance ... demand from your grocer the particular brand of treacle Fowler imports from the West Indies. Use no other, or your purchase of Brown Barbados will have been in vain ... buy a 1-pound tin of Mr. Fowler's treacle and allow its contents to subside in a saucepan ... and when it is lukewarm you must add to it one tablespoon of Old Jamaica rum ..."

Others have added cologne, fruit, or flower extracts, stale urine, dead fish, or even dung (but, although many butterflies are attracted to excrement, *Catocala* generally avoid it). Sargent adds elderberry wine to his mixture; Winter included bananas; and in Westport, Connecticut, Yale entomologist Lawrence Gall applies beer, honey, and molasses with the kind of garden sprayer normally used to apply the stuff that kills bugs rather than feeds them. One particularly dedicated enthusiast, Louisiana lepidopterist Vernon Brou, published a recipe calling for 400–600 apples or peaches, 55 pounds of sugar, and 10 gallons of beer, fermented for two weeks in a 55-gallon drum. ("He thinks big," said Gall. When he traps moths with lights, "his light traps look like lunar landing gear.")

Whatever brew you use, patches the size of your hand applied by paintbrush on tree trunks or fence posts are sure to attract underwings. (Wait till the sun goes down or it will attract hornets, also.) Remember, though, this stuff ferments. "Explosion of a jar of sticky bait on the back seat of a car, or anywhere else, can be most distressing," Winter noted. Bring a flashlight, and cover the lens with a yellow paper napkin to avoid disturbing the moths as they feed.

One final warning: in the excitement of the chase, don't wander onto private property in the night without prior permission. "Landowners seeing lights moving slowly through their woodlots at night have been known to investigate with showers of shotgun pellets," Winter warned.

But you may encounter more welcome surprises as you search for moths in the dark woods. A friend of Winter's, out sugaring one night, thought he felt a hand clap onto his shoulder, and next expected an angry landowner's gun-barrel in the ribs. He turned to face his fate—and stared into the face of a flying squirrel, who had landed on his shoulder.

Autumn

Hatchling Snappers

Ulysseses of Our Day

*T*heir story began some 200 million years ago, when ferns grew as tall as trees and dragonflies grew big as crows, before the dinosaurs. Their journey begins anew each fall as they emerge from the sandy soils of lawns, gardens, fields, golf courses, and ballfields, from the sandbanks by the sides of roads and the sand stored in piles at public works departments.

Here, one-inch eggs, round and white as ping-pong balls, have waited beneath the sun-warmed soil since early June. Here the little lives curled inside them have grown, preparing for this dangerous, dramatic moment: the time when the hatchling snapping turtles break out of their eggshells, dig out of their nests, and begin the perilous, often circuitous journey towards ponds, marshes, rivers, and scrub swamps. Many never make it. Those that do can take up to a week.

Thoreau, recording his observations of snappers in 1854, compared their journeys to Ulysses' decades-long return home in *The Iliad*. No one today knows their epic journeys better than David Carroll, Burroughs Award–winning author of *The Year of the Turtle*. He has been chronicling the lives of New England's turtles for four decades.

Of New England's ten species of freshwater turtles, snappers are the only ones you are likely to see as hatchlings, Carroll explains. Snappers are among the commonest turtles in North America and they often hatch near our homes.

Baby snappers look just like the adults, only in miniature, with big heads, hooked jaws, and tails as long as their unadorned, flattish, dark shells. Sometimes you'll find them so freshly hatched they still sport an egg tooth, the protrusion at the tip of the upper jaw that helped them hatch out of the egg. (The babies even smell like old eggs.) You'll often see a protrusion on the belly, too—just where you'd find a stumpy navel if this were a newborn human child. This is the remnant of the yolk sac which nourished the baby turtle in the egg.

Even at this tender age, snappers are tough critters, facing an almost incredibly tough task.

"These hatchling snappers are so strong and brave, you won't believe it," Carroll says as he explores the sandy soils of the mosaic of wetlands, pine uplands, and old fields that he calls "the digs"—where he knows he will find turtle nests.

Just by the simple act of hatching, baby turtles have already surmounted enormous odds. Some experts estimate that 90 percent of snappers' nests are raided by predators. In the sandy soils shaded only by the purple seedheads of bluestem grass, the leathery leaves of sweetfern, and the short, golden blossoms of gray goldenrod, everywhere he finds little craters where a hungry skunk or raccoon has excavated a turtle nest for a high-protein snack. Empty eggshells strew the entrance, making the nest look "like a robbed temple," as Carroll says,

"A single family of skunks can wipe out many nests of turtles," he points out. Often, though, the marauders don't dig up all the eggs at once, but come back for seconds. A few weeks back, Carroll came across several such nests, rescued some of the eggs, and took them home for hatching.

The babies leave eggshells in the nest when they hatch, he explains. You can easily tell a hatched-out nest from one that's been robbed: the successful nest will show no eggshells. The babies leave only a tiny, two-inch exit hole at the base of the mount of soil where their mother dug her nest.

As soon as its head pokes out of the ground, the baby snapper "already thrusts forth its tremendous head—for the first time in this sphere," wrote Thoreau, "and slowly moves from side to side—opening its small glistening eyes for the first time to the light ... as if it had endured the trials of this world for a century."

Or perhaps the hatchling is considering the trials of its immediate future: a gauntlet of birds, skunks, dogs, snakes, cats, raccoons, weasels, children, and cars.

And that's only on the way to water. There, more dangers lurk: bullfrogs, pickerel, other snappers.

"Almost anyone can eat them," says Carroll. And unlike sea-turtle hatchlings, who make a beeline from nest to sea, a snapper may explore land for more than a week before settling into the pond or swamp that will become its home. Carroll believes the hatchlings undertake these perilous wanderings for a reason: they are mapping their world, committing it to memory.

So don't interfere with a baby's journey, Carroll advises, except in one instance: If you spot one crossing a road or parking lot, pick it up and help it across.

Don't do this with an adult snapper. Their powerful, hooked jaws can break a broomstick. The other end can do damage, too. With strong feet and sharp nails, a big snapper will grab your hand and draw your skin across the serrated back edge of the shell like a crosscut saw. "It's best to redirect traffic (not the turtle) if possible," Carroll advises.

Even though a baby snapper won't bite, if you look at its cross-shaped plastron, or undershell, you'll see why the adults do. Most turtles' hard plastrons cover the whole belly, leaving only modest openings for the leathery legs and neck. But the snapper's plastron looks like a thong bathing suit. This risqué design is why a snapper can't pull itself into its shell to hide, and why it needs defensive weapons.

"They're not passive resisters," says Carroll.

And snappers are extraordinarily agile. Even the giants—wild snappers can live for seventy years or more and grow to more than fifty pounds—can move with astonishing speed. The Audubon Society's *Field Guide to North American Reptiles* notes that snappers displaced two miles from home returned within a few hours. Carroll found one of these fast-moving giants a few years back with a shell as large as a warrior's shield.

"For every one of the great ones people gasp at, maybe a couple hundred of the little guys have disappeared," Carroll says.

During a survey of "the digs," he spots perhaps fifty turtle nests—almost all of them ravaged by predators, probably skunks. But predators are the least of the turtles' problems. Pavement is the real curse.

"As long as there's habitat, there'll be turtles," Carroll says. "If we left more land alone, it would be fine. But we don't because every inch has to earn a profit, or pay a tax, or support a person."

But "the digs"—for the moment—is safe. So are the eight rescued hatchlings Carroll has brought from home to release here.

Only a few paces away from other snappers' nests, near a marsh nearly choked with burr reed and cattail—perfect cover in which a nestling could hide—he opens his palm and lets the first one go.

"That little brain has a couple of hundred million years of history programmed into it," Carroll says as the hatchling crawls from his palm and scurries into the undergrowth near the marsh. The little turtle pauses, head erect, eyes unblinking, "as if it had endured the trials of this world for a century."

"Good luck," Carroll says softly. He turns back towards his car, and man and turtle go their separate ways.

Milkweed

A Wonder to Wish On

☙

*W*hen she was a child, Selinda Chiquoine loved visiting her grandmother in the Catskills. In the last days of summer, she used to cross the creek near her grandmother's house to a field full of marvelous plants that grew taller than her dad. The thick leathery leaves and hairy stems oozed a white sap, giving the plant its name: milkweed. But the best part of the milkweed, the part that she and her brother came to pick, was the tapering, warty green pods, up to four inches long, which ripen in late September and fill the autumn air with downy fluff.

A milkweed pod provides a child's treasure chest of toys: the two curved halves of the woody outer layer make "fairy cradles." The cradles can be bedded with some of the downy seeds inside. But since there are more than 450 parachuting seeds inside each pod, there are more than enough to blow about—and as every child knows, if you catch and then release a floating seed, any wish you make upon it will come true.

Chiquoine and her brother used to bring many dozens of the pods back to their grandmother's porch and, amid a blizzard of unmanageable fluff, extract the flat, match-size woody part (called the gynostegium) to which the parachuting seeds adhere. They would stuff them into tins, pretending they were packing sardines.

"It's a great kids' plant," says Jack Sanders, author of the 1993 book *Hedgemaids and Fairy Candles: The Lives and Lore of*

North American Wildflowers. He and his childhood friends used to blow the milkweed seeds into each other's faces, and on family vacations on Nantucket, he used the pods as fishing lures: they are a natural float, after all. "Sometimes," he said, "they even worked."

But milkweed's wonders extend beyond childhood whimsy, as Chiquoine, now a professional gardener and co-owner of Flowers Anonymous in Sharon, New Hampshire, well knows. Milkweeds thrive in her flower garden, and she allows any that show up in the vegetable patch to stay.

"What was once safely considered a weed," Chiquoine notes wryly, "is now in the perennial garden." She keeps them for their dense, rounded heads of rose, lavender, pink, and soft brownish purple flowers, which exude a honeysuckle-sweet fragrance.

According to Bill Cullina, nursery manager and propagator at the New England Wild Flower Society, some of the milkweed species, including whorled milkweed, purple milkweed, and butterfly weed, are so "garden-worthy" that the Society offers them for sale at its Garden in the Woods in Framingham, Massachusetts and sells the seeds through its January catalog.

A growing number of gardeners covet these plants because they attract an astounding array of hummingbirds, bees, and most of all, butterflies—some of whom, notably the monarchs, emerge from their chrysalises in the fall, many of them on or near the milkweed plants.

"Milkweed, among the native plants that we have, is one of the most amazing—and until recently, one of the most overlooked," Sanders said in an interview from his home in Ridgefield, Connecticut. Not that milkweed has, until now, been ignored: as he points out in his book, the earliest American colonists stuffed pillows and mattresses with the seed hairs. They mixed this material with flax and wool to yield a silky thread for sewing. Later, in the 19th century, people made cloth, hats, and paper from the fiber.

In World War II, when there was a shortage of Asian kapok, milkweed down provided the stuffing in life preservers and the linings of airmen's jackets. Yet today, many agricultural agencies list milkweed as a noxious weed—especially in pastures, because livestock won't eat it, and its long taproots make it difficult to dig up.

But Native Americans long appreciated milkweed, and recognized the more than seventy-five different American species centuries before scientists made up different names for them. (The milkweed family has more than two thousand species, most of them tropical. New England has eight.) The Sioux boiled the young seed pods and ate them with buffalo meat. (Esclepain, a chemical constituent of all the milkweed species, makes a good meat tenderizer.) The Chippewa stewed the flowers of one species to make jam. Hopi mothers ate another kind to stimulate the flow of milk for their nursing babies. Canadian tribes boiled the young shoots and ate them like asparagus.

Eating a big batch of milkweed is not a good idea if you don't know what you're doing. Not only does milkweed have poisonous look-alikes (like dogbane); some milkweeds contain dangerous levels of bitter toxins, which can be removed by covering the harvested plant with boiling water and boiling it over and over again. But these very toxins make milkweed an important medicinal plant—and a resource to which milkweed-eating caterpillars and their butterflies have marvelously adapted.

Milkweed's medicinal properties are honored in the plants' family name: The Asclepiadaceae are named for Asclepius, the mythical son of the Greek god Apollo, who became the first great physician. (Asclepius gave the medical profession its symbol, the caduceus, from the wise serpents who coiled around his staff and told him the cures for diseases. The snakes' advice was so sound Asclepius was soon raising the dead, until an irate Zeus incinerated him with a lightning bolt for being a show-off.)

The milky juice of the milkweeds is full of chemicals that profoundly affect the human body. In the late 19th century, American physicians used extracts of milkweed to treat the symptoms of smallpox, colds, flus, dyspepsia, indigestion, and breathing problems. Among the milkweeds' chemical constituents are cardiac glycosides, which stimulate the heart. Today these compounds are used to re-start ailing hearts after surgery.

Humans are not the only species to make use of milkweeds' powerful chemicals. Certain insects figured it out millions of years before we did. Mammals and most leaf-munching insects are repelled by milkweeds' poisons, but some have adapted to use them in their own defense. Caterpillars of the butterfly genus *Danaidae*, the most well known of which is the orange and black monarch, feed almost exclusively on milkweeds. A particular favorite is the showy, orange-flowering butterfly weed. The plant's juice makes both the caterpillar and the butterfly so distasteful that birds will vomit for half an hour after eating one—and most who try it never bother those species again.

In late summer and early fall, look for the jade-green chrysalis of the monarch, flecked with dots of gold, on milkweed plants and the low branches of shrubs and trees near them. In nine to twelve days, this beautiful case changes from jade to teal to brown, and finally you can see the orange and black wings of the butterfly about to emerge within.

The adult emerges with wings folded, hanging head down while it pumps its wings with fluid—a process that takes about twenty minutes. It won't fly for another hour or so as the wings harden, so don't touch or disturb it, or the wings might deform. In early fall, New England's newly emerged monarchs immediately head south, traveling at the speed of a quick jogger, sometimes covering up to eighty miles a day. They feast on the nectar of still-blooming milkweeds along the way.

Their destination: the highlands of northern Mexico. (But there, unfortunately for the insects, some birds have learned how to outsmart the butterflies' chemical defense. Grosbeaks and orioles there avoid the poisonous parts, eschewing the wings and skinning the butterflies, eating the insides only.) Our fall butterflies' progeny will return to New England in the spring—where in fields, along roadsides, and now increasingly, in gardens, they'll find plenty of milkweed to nourish the generations to come.

Mysteries of the
Monarchs' Migration

☙

*A*uthor and ecologist Robert Michael Pyle calls it "the sky river." Each fall and spring, wave after wave of flapping orange and black and white butterflies begin to pour over the North American landscape, flying between forty and one hundred miles per day.

The sky river, Pyle explains, runs two ways: north with spring and south with the fall. The migration of North America's monarchs is the greatest butterfly spectacle on the planet. All these beautiful, large butterflies share a common goal: they are all heading, en masse like birds, on a migration of hundreds or thousands of miles that none of them has ever before undertaken.

How these featherlight insects accomplish this long-distance feat is a mystery that has tantalized naturalists for centuries. Until recently, nearly everything about them was unknown. Where most of the monarchs—most of those east of the Rockies—spend the winter, among forested slopes west of Mexico City, was only discovered in 1975, thanks to forty years of butterfly tagging efforts initiated by Dr. Fred Urquhart of Toronto and collaborators. Debate still continues over the exact routes the insects take and how long the monarchs have been doing this (some say the trip is a response to post-settlement deforestation).

One University of California biologist, Adrien Wenner, even contends they don't migrate; he argues they are merely expanding and contracting their range, as many other butterflies do.

Naturalist and author Edwin Way Teale considered the migration of the monarch "one of the most puzzling features of American seasons." Four decades later, Pyle writes, it puzzles still. "Confronted with thousands, or millions, of big, flapping, soaring, gliding, sucking creatures clearly going somewhere," he writes, "we stand in awe."

Lately, though, scientists have done much more than stand there. To penetrate the mysteries of the monarch migration, they have tracked monarchs with radar, subjected them to magnets and jet-lag in experiments, and affixed millions of tiny tags to the insects' forewings in hopes of recovering them and revealing their routes.

A few autumns ago, Pyle decided to go one step further: he followed them. On foot and in his car, for 9,462 miles over 57 days, the Washington state ecologist traveled with monarchs from their northernmost breeding grounds in British Columbia down to their wintering grounds in Mexico and California.

His chronicle of the experience, *Chasing Monarchs: Migrating with the Butterflies of Passage,* comes on the heels of a number of startling new discoveries about the monarchs' migration—and the threats to its survival. Despite two decades of international proclamations calling for their protection, today, America's most beloved butterflies are under siege. Threats range from illegal logging in their Mexican wintering ground to toxic pollen from gene-spliced corn to a trendy new way to celebrate weddings. Says Pyle, "the migratory butterflies are in worse trouble than ever."

On his two-month journey, he saw many of these threats first-hand. He bedded down with them and rose with them. As they floated on thermals, he followed beneath in his 1982 Honda. Sometimes he lost them in butterfly-barren landscapes, where pesticides poison their primary food plant, the milkweed. When he lost track of them, he would head in the direction in which the last one he had seen had vanished. He watched them dodge swallows and dragonflies, saw them hit by cars. But he also observed in these delicate-looking insects an astonishing resiliency, plasticity, and individuality, and something which, if it were observed in humans, could only be called an iron will.

"As I watched this perfect monarch steadying herself to sail on," he wrote of one butterfly he observed, "facing a journey of a thousand miles or more, I had to believe that there was a little more of something like freedom built into her system than the rigid lines drawn on migration maps seem to allow. Nothing so refined as freedom as we think of it—but the freedom, nonetheless, to respond to the vagaries and gifts of the days with every adaptive tool and option that kindly evolution has provided."

Some ingenious experiments are now revealing how migrating monarchs use some of these adaptive tools in remarkably sophisticated ways. For, although butterflies can and do learn—Pyle has seen them learn and remember the exact location of individual nectar plants—this ability can't help them find their way, for none of them have ever been there before. The butterflies who head south from New England, for example, are the great-grandchildren, or great-great-grandchildren, or even great-great-great-grandchildren of the ones who made the trip last year. And although these individuals overwinter in Mexico or California, few of them, if any, ever make it back to their birthplace in the spring, and none of them survive to make the trip south again in the fall.

Spring's migrants have overwintered by the millions on trees confined to a few hundred hectares in Mexico and California. Their orange wings literally cover the boughs. On the way north, in the spring, they will mate and lay hundreds of pinhead-size eggs on milkweeds. The eggs will hatch into black, ivory, and yellow caterpillars who grow so quickly they split their skins five times in a month. In middle and late summer the caterpillars are encased in jewelbox-like chrysalises hanging from milkweed plants, waiting to emerge as orange and black beauties. And when they emerge, they continue the journey.

How, then, do they navigate? For years, researchers wondered whether they, like birds, used a sun compass, but efforts to prove this consistently failed. A sun compass requires that creatures compensate for time by shifting direction relative to the changing azimuth of the sun. To test the hypothesis, researchers have tried shifting that clock by six hours under artificial lights, essentially giving their bodies jet-lag, and then releasing the butterflies to see if their bearing changed from south/southwest to north/northwest. But upon release, the butterflies zigzagged in all directions.

This is exactly the problem Sandra Perez, now an assistant professor of biology at the University of Texas in El Paso, and her colleagues encountered when they began similar experiments at the University of Kansas. Perez recognized the erratic flight: rather than an indicator of its migratory bearing, "the butterfly is escaping imminent death from a large predator," she explained. In later experiments, they tried to allow the butterflies to calm down. They refrigerated them, so they were unable to fly at first release. The jet-lagged insects warmed up as they calmed down. Now they no longer flew erratically, but they didn't fly south/southwest or north/northwest. The vanishing bearing, the team found, was always in the direction the wind blew.

But Perez knew her study animal. "In animals you haven't cooled down, the head is in the direction they want to go" she noted. "That is the thing that told us the story." Testing more than four hundred individual monarchs, the researchers recorded the direction the warming insects' tiny heads were facing as they disappeared over the horizon. The clock-shifted butterflies headed, as predicted, north/northwest—just as they would have if they were using a sun compass.

The sun compass may be even more sophisticated than first imagined. Lincoln Brower, a research professor of biology at Sweet Briar College in Virginia, suspects that the butterflies' internal clock allows them to adjust their course by one degree per day. Thanks to new methods of charting the monarchs' course, it now appears that they do not migrate in a roughly straight line, but a curved one. Besides affixing tiny tags to the butterflies' wings, Brower and others can now chemically fingerprint butterflies to discover where they have come from. All monarch caterpillars eat milkweed, a plant with an acrid latex containing potent cardiac glycosides, causing birds who eat them to vomit and later to remember to avoid them. These chemicals differ among different species of milkweed, some of which grow only in certain parts of the country, so chemically testing the butterflies helps plot their travels. From these methods, it now appears that on the return journey north, for instance, many Mexican-hibernating butterflies use their adjustable sun compass and internal clock to head due north until they hit Texas, lay eggs there, and their offspring then follow an increasingly eastern bearing, heading to Indiana, and then arriving in New England around July.

But the sun doesn't shine every day. Researchers have long suspected that migrating creatures must rely on a variety of cues, and researchers had earlier published theories that butterflies also use the Earth's magnetic field to verify their bearings. Perez and her colleagues completed experiments exposing butterflies to strong artificial magnetic fields. Their results lend further support to this idea.

They also seem to follow topographic clues, Pyle discovered. His migrants tended to follow rivers and sometimes highways, for these areas lead to the nectar-bearing plants the butterflies sip for fuel, the milkweeds and butterfly weeds that tend to grow in abandoned fields and meadows. He migrated with them along "nectar corridors," down the Columbia, Snake, Bear, and Colorado rivers, and then through Hell's Canyon and the Grand Canyon to Mexico—and there found that yet another theory about their migration does not always hold true. "The Rockies were thought to be the Berlin Wall of monarchs," he said. Ever since the discovery of the Mexican wintering grounds in the cool highlands of Michoacan, it has been thought that all eastern monarchs headed here, and all western monarchs wintered in southern California. He found that some western monarchs fly from northwest to southeast and at least some enter Mexico.

Further complicating a complex picture, not all butterflies stay on their intended course. Hundreds, perhaps thousands, are blown by winds out to sea; some have landed on research vessels and oil derricks. Some hitchhikers make it all the way to England and Bermuda.

Many millions die along the way. Reviewing records going back to 1880, "it's clear that monarchs along the Atlantic seaboard have fluctuated dramatically over the years," Brower says. Monarch population levels fluctuate far more dramatically than those of birds, says Victor Demasi. A research affiliate in entomology at Yale-Peabody Museum in New Haven, Connecticut, he has worked with the census organization Monarch Watch to mark and release up to 760 monarchs in one 30-day period, working two hours per day. Some years, within the same time frame, he has found and released only fifteen. Nine years of census records from Cape May, New Jersey, counting butterflies migrating from September 1 to October 30 show numbers of butterflies can fluctuate from a spectacular average of 142 per hour on average (in 1995) to 10 per hour in 1996. None of these fluctuations seem to correlate directly with any one cause, nor do they hold true throughout monarchs' extensive range.

Despite increasing interest in the monarch, the species' secrets remain as elusive as a butterfly on the wind. "We have no integrated database, period," says Pyle. Which makes the plethora of threats now facing the monarch even more worrisome, he says, "because many of these factors simply haven't been looked at in the past."

"There is a certain toughness to the butterfly, and they can thrive in human-altered habitat," Pyle said. But "monarchs need an absence of direct toxins; a plenitude of milkweed, and a plenitude of nectar sources. All are potentially weak links." And all are under assault, some flagrant, some insidious.

"Clearly the primary thing to worry about, the Achilles heel of the migration, is protecting the Mexican wintering ground," asserts Brower. As a result of a Mexican presidential decree issued under international pressure in 1986, 16,100 hectares of forested highland were to be protected or partially protected in Michoacan to safeguard the eastern population's wintering ground. But new surveys show that some of these areas contained no butterflies, while some unprotected areas contained colonies of fifty to sixty million. Worse, illegal logging continues even in protected areas. Results of a new study backed by GIS data, redefining and expanding the area requiring protection, was presented to the government of Mexico, Brower said, and he hopes the Mexican embassy will be deluged with letters supporting increased protection. Meanwhile, development still threatens the California wintering sites as well.

And as the monarchs' winter sanctuaries dwindle, so do their caterpillars' summer nurseries and the adults' nectar corridors. Not only are their food plants uprooted and poisoned to make way for crops and homes; the caterpillars are also victims of insecticides intended for crop-eating caterpillars. Augmenting agriculture's already deadly arsenal of sprayed poisons is a new threat of unknown proportions: toxic pollen. By splicing genes from a soil bacterium (Bt) into corn, agricultural biotechnologists developed a crop that manufactures its own caterpillar-killing pesticide. Cornell University entomologist John Losey reports that 50 percent of monarch caterpillars die when they eat milkweeds that have become dusted with bt-corn pollen. A National Academy of Sciences survey published earlier reported that 50 percent of North America's monarchs breed in the Corn Belt. And some 25 percent of the American corn crop is now planted with Bt.

"This is an example of how wrong unanticipated things can go," says Brower. "What is the straw that will break the camel's back? That is my concern."

Even seemingly well-meaning gestures may have sinister consequences for the migrating monarchs. A new trend of celebrating weddings with the release of dozens of captive-reared butterflies could spread disease as well as damage their natural genetics. And this unfortunate fad also "threatens to warp our collective picture of the species," writes Pyle in his book. "As tens of thousands of monarchs are released far from their birthplaces, the sum will amount to increasingly unreliable maps."

For this reason, he, as well as the nation's major butterfly conservation organizations, recommends that teachers eschew purchasing butterfly kits for the classroom. Instead, he suggests, take the children outside. Find the caterpillars. Safeguard their milkweeds locally. "Butterflies don't come from a box," he reminds us after following the wild, free-flying beasts for more than 9,000 miles. "We have to keep in mind the joy of these animals—experience the serenity and even the ecstasy of personal contact with the actual, wild animals."

Voices of Courage in the Night

ॐ

*H*alf an hour after sunset, they begin moving in waves. Protected by the darkness, guided by the stars, millions of tiny songbirds pass over our rooftops, flying invisibly through the night.

The dark hides these fragile fliers from predators like hawks, who migrate by day. The evenings' cool, stable air smoothes their flyways. But, to bird watchers' frustration, night also shrouds the miracle of these songbirds' migration.

Sometimes you can catch a glimpse of their silhouettes against the full moon. Some ornithologists have guessed at their numbers by counting birds as they fly though the beam of a powerful searchlight, or counting them with radar. Unfortunately, these methods only tell you how many birds are flying, not what species they are, because they can't be clearly seen.

But they can be clearly heard. Each species' call is as distinctive as its plumage. If you lie awake autumn nights and listen, you can hear their voices.

Bill Evans has been doing this for more than a dozen years.

"It's just incredible," says the Cornell-based researcher. "You get in touch with these little guys flying to South America. It's so fun to hear them talking back and forth in the night."

Five thousand birds may fly through a one-mile cross-section in a single night, and most fall migrants in New England fly beneath 2,000 feet. Their calls come through loud and clear, even in the city. (Your ear can easily filter out car and jet noise. In fact, if you climb to the roof of a tall building, you can hear the birds' voices even better.)

Evans says cloudy nights are often best for listening, especially after a cold front has passed through. A gentle northwesterly wind will carry even more species towards the coast.

You are likely to hear very distinct basic call types. Twinkly, short, high call notes—like a single cricket chirp—belong to the warblers and sparrows. The lower calls—like the note of a spring peeper—belong to the thrushes, including the robins, as they migrate to South and Central America.

You may even be able to pick out individual voices, which are as distinctive as our own. If so, you can track that individual as it flies overhead, until its call recedes into the night.

Flying in loose flocks—each bird spaced hundreds of feet from the next—they call to one another to stay in contact. Perhaps the calls serve as air traffic control, to keep birds who can't see one another from colliding. Or perhaps they call as we might whistle in the dark: to bolster their confidence during a long and dangerous journey.

"You realize you can live the journeys these birds are making, the miraculousness of it," Evans says. "You can visualize all those birds going over without seeing a thing."

Evans first realized the scientific potential of his night time eavesdropping when he was a student at the University of Minnesota in 1985. An avid birder, he was camped on a bluff overlooking the St. Croix River, awaiting the spring migration. As he lay in his sleeping bag one night, he picked out a familiar voice: the black-billed cuckoo, a secretive bird sometimes heard but seldom seen. "If I had tried to find them during the day, I would be lucky to find two or three," he said. But then the voice came again—and again. In the dark, the invisible had been made plain. Within an hour he heard more than a hundred cuckoos passing overhead.

"It was like a vision," he remembers. "I literally said right then: that's what I'm going to do with my life for a long time to come. I'm going to record these night flight calls to make acoustic documents for the future, to monitor bird populations for conservation."

The day after his epiphany, Evans began to configure the gear to make and analyze his recordings. Today he uses much the same equipment: a microphone built from a plastic dinner plate, a hearing aid microphone, some wire, and a 9-volt battery, connected to a cassette deck and a hi-fi VCR.

Mounting his mikes on rooftops, barns, and platforms in cornfields, he can record for nine hours on the videotape. On a good night he can collect ten thousand individual call notes.

These nocturnal calls are often quite different from the territorial songs birds sing in spring. In fact, most nighttime calls consist of only a single note, a type of call which may be infrequent during the day.

When Evans first came to Cornell's Laboratory of Ornithology in 1987, he discovered that none of these birds' nighttime calls were recorded in the institution's respected library of natural sounds. He had to identify the calls himself—a task which, to a less dedicated birder, might have seemed impossible. How to match a nighttime call with an unseen bird? "If you point your perception at a problem, you gain knowledge," he says. Take the night call of the wood thrush, for instance: Evans had heard it many times at night, and wondered whose voice it was. Then one afternoon in 1989, in Ithaca, he was walking down a dirt road and heard the note again, this time in between the phrases of the wood thrush's flute-like, fluttered song.

After more than a decade of careful listening, Evans has amassed a personal aural field guide to nearly all the warbler and sparrow species in eastern North America, as well as all of the migratory thrushes. A series of mellow whistles tells him a flood of rose-breasted grosbeaks are passing through. Wood thrush migration calls sound somewhat like the chime of a bedspring. Swainson's thrushes sound like spring peepers. Red-breasted nuthatches call "Yank! Yank!" A dry "schleip," $1/20$ of a second long, signals the Canada warbler. In this way, Evans has pioneered a major new technique to measure, for the first time, which species are migrating where and when.

"It's a really cutting-edge way to get another view of migration," says Wayne Petersen, Massachusetts Audubon Society's ornithologist. "He's quantifying a whole new way of looking at nighttime migration. It's great stuff."

"I think it's outstanding work," says Don Kroodsma, an expert on bird communication and professor of biology at the University of Massachusetts, Amherst. "The potential for this work is just extraordinary."

Using his techniques, for the first time, ornithologists may be able to map precise migratory times and routes for individual species, as well as monitor dips and rises in population.

Evans has set up recording stations at seven locations in New York State, as well as in Texas, Illinois, and Florida. From his analysis of these recordings, he knows, for instance, that rose-breasted grosbeaks are more common migrants over the eastern half of New York State and that they tend to drop out of the sky to rest by 3 a.m. But grey-cheeked thrushes and upland sandpipers, both species headed to South America, are more common migrants over western New York and tend to migrate all night long.

Acoustic monitoring can't solve all the mysteries of songbird migration; for one thing, not all migratory songbird species call at night. Vireos appear to pass over silently. No one has ever heard a nighttime call from a flycatcher. But Evans foresees broad applications: perhaps one day microphone stations will stretch all across North America. Birders and researchers might be able to plug into the Internet and follow the migrations of their favorite species aurally on their computers.

And meanwhile, you can still enjoy the nighttime voices the old-fashioned way. Just listen.

Swarming Ladybugs

The Take-Over of the Asian Multi-Colored

৯৫

A reporter once asked British geneticist J.B.S. Haldane what the famed biologist could discern about the Almighty from a lifetime of studying Creation. Haldane is said to have replied that God must have "an inordinate fondness for beetles."

If his observation is correct, then Someone up there must be delirious with joy on warm early-fall days. That's when much of the Northeast is literally crawling with beetles.

Fortunately, these are beneficial and highly popular beetles: cheerful, round, orange and black spotted ladybugs.

They are, however, not acting like ladybugs normally act. They're flitting around on warm, sunlit afternoons by the hundreds, making it look like the air is dancing with spots. They're congregating on light-colored, south-facing buildings to take advantage of the sun. They're covering white clapboards with upward-crawling polka-dots. Except at Tom Kemp's house in Milton, Massachusetts, where they stuck to the paint he'd just applied. "These bugs are great at eating unwanted insects," Kemp said, "but they don't make great siding."

No, our favorite beetles have not all gone mad. These are ladybugs of a species fairly new to our shores—and for the multicolored Asian lady beetle, this is perfectly normal behavior.

The ladybugs are mostly looking for a way to get into your attic, where they would like to sleep through the winter. But many of them, confused by the indoor warmth, remain in people's living spaces, landing in the gravy boat, crawling over the birthday cake, flying into the bathwater, gathering unhappily at the windows.

Many people are still delighted to see them—but not everyone. Not the types who call up Natalia Vanderberg. At the Department of Agriculture's Systematic Entomology Lab in Washington, Vanderberg got a call from a guy who wanted the government to fly over his town and spray it.

"Some people are just freaking out," reports Brian Fitzek, spokesman for the Entomological Society of America, a fellow whose job doesn't normally bring him much fan mail. And in *Countryside and Small Stock Journal*, a headline reads, "Ladybug, ladybug, fly away home / Get out of my house, and leave me alone!"

The beetles' behavior would be considered decidedly unladybuglike by most of the 475 species native to North America. Most of them migrate, and many overwinter in clusters. Others tuck away singly. Many of us unknowingly shelter a ladybug or two in our attics. But none of our native ladybugs swarm en masse into houses. The multicolored Asian lady beetle (*Harmonia axyridis*) thinks nothing of it.

The Asians may range in color from yellow to orange to red, and a few are black with orange dots. The number of dots also varies; there may be none, or there may be as many as sixteen. But what's most distinctive about this foreign import is its voracious appetite for the aphids that attack fruit trees. For just that reason, the USDA tried introducing the Asian beetles into this country several times since 1914—but the beetles never seemed to take, so the scientists finally gave up.

Then in the summer of 1988, Louisiana state entomologists found Asian beetles thriving just outside New Orleans—hundreds of miles from where they had been released, but near a major shipping port where beetles could easily have arrived as stowaways. So most biologists think these ladybugs got here on their own.

Ever since, they've been spreading in all directions.

"I suspect they'll be in every state of the union soon," predicted research entomologist Louis Tedders of Georgia, shortly after the beetles arrived. And as far as orchardists are considered, that's great news. Few farmers don't welcome ladybugs. Their very name honors our gratitude to them. During the Middle Ages, European farms prayed to the Blessed Virgin Mary to end the plagues of pests on their crops. When the cheery orange beetles arrived in response, grateful supplicants named the insects "Our Lady beetle."

The multicoloreds are an exceptional boon to fruit tree growers. They prefer the aphids that congregate on pecan, plum, peach, apple, maple, and pine trees, as well as the insects that plague ornamental roses. And they're exceptionally voracious: before it reaches adulthood, a single Asian multicolored will eat more than three hundred of the soft-bodied aphids. (All ladybug babies, by the way, are blackish grubs with yellow, orange, or red spots, shaped, as Vanderberg describes them, "like baby crocodiles with six legs." Rather like caterpillars, lady beetle grubs create chrysalis-like pupal cases that eventually hatch out the familiar orange and black adult form.)

At the U.S. Agricultural Research Service's Southeastern Fruit and Nut Tree Research Laboratory in Byron, Georgia, Tedders reports that since the new species showed up, some pecan growers have cut pesticide use by 50–75 percent. "A lot of the pecan growers down here have been able to eliminate pesticides for aphids completely," he said.

And there's more good news: the foreign beetles show no signs of usurping any native ladies. According to Tedders' research, since the Asians' appearance, native numbers are actually increasing. One reason for this may be that the *Harmonia* species seems to be displacing an earlier-imported European species, the seven-spotted, which had been displacing the common native convergent lady beetle, says Tedders.

That the multicolored got established here on its own was one surprise. That it likes to come into people's houses was another. U.S. scientists knew that these ladybugs overwintered in cracks among sun-drenched limestone, marble, and granite outcroppings; they never realized the bugs would try to get inside people's homes. But in Asia, homeowners have long been willing to share their homes with the beetles. "In Japan, in fact, people are honored to have these ladybugs stay in the house," Tedders says. Still, he's now researching ways to keep them out of the homes of less-tolerant Americans. One way, he suggests wryly, is to paint your house black, as they are only attracted to light-colored buildings.

Some particularly unhappy homeowners have tried to scrape the ladybugs off their walls, or worse, smooshed them. This only makes things worse (especially from the ladybugs' point of view), because it showcases a wonder of ladybug physiology: all ladybugs can exude a foul-smelling yellow liquid from their elbows. This is actually their blood, and you'll see and smell a lot more of it if you smoosh one. P.S.: It stains.

So don't bug the lady beetles. Meanwhile, if you're feeling overrun, some suggestions:

Gather them up and take them to a greenhouse. The owners will be thrilled.

Or keep them over the winter in a jar in your refrigerator. Use a porous cap so they don't suffocate. Every few weeks, take the jar out, let the beetles warm up, and offer a sponge soaked in sugar-water for their refreshment.

The ladybugs left at large will probably settle down in a few days. You'll see them again in the spring trying to get out. Just open the window and let them fly away home.

Effects of a Sparse Acorn Year

෨

*L*ittle furry bodies streak across the roads as fast as drops of rainwater across a windshield. Especially in the fall, your morning commute to work can seem like a living obstacle course.

Every autumn has its share of suicidal squirrels and kamikaze chipmunks. But some years are worse than others. Forester William Guenther of Windham County, Vermont remembers a year when "I got to the point where I wouldn't even veer off the road any more for a squirrel. I'd just get killed trying to save them."

What makes these critters throng the roadways in certain years? Possibly for the same reason you might be seeing fewer blue jays, but many deer and lots of wild turkeys.

In a word, the answer is acorns.

More accurately, two words: No acorns.

Some years acorns are so abundant that "walking through the woods is like walking on a field of ball bearings," says Jack Witham, a University of Maine researcher studying the seed crop at Holt Research Forest in Arrowsic. He should know: he collects and analyzes 264 seed traps in the 100-acre study area of this pine-oak woods each year.

The years they're abundant are good ones for wildlife. "Acorns are a highly concentrated, high-fat food for many animal species," explains John McDonald, a wildlife biologist and deer specialist with the Massachusetts Division of Fish and Wildlife. The medieval English so valued acorns for fattening swine that anyone who destroyed an oak was fined according to the size of the tree and its history of bearing fruit. Acorns provided a winter staple for North America's earliest peoples, probably since Paleolithic times.

Many rodents rely on acorns. One naturalist calculated that a single chipmunk could gather nine hundred acorns a day. Jays relish them, too, opening the hard shell by holding it with their feet and hammering it with their sharp beaks. Grouse, pheasants, and wood ducks swallow them whole. Bears also love them. White deer concentrate near acorn bonanzas. Even carnivores like fox and raccoon eat acorns.

But in years acorns are scarce, the animals need to search out alternative larder.

Oaks, like many trees, fruit in cycles. Some years acorns are plentiful, others they're scarce. Drought plays a role, too. All of it is perfectly natural, and animals, assures Wayne Petersen, Massachusetts Audubon's ornithologist, "have evolved strategies to cope with this very nicely."

This doesn't mean birds and squirrels wouldn't appreciate some extra cracked corn or sunflowers at the feeder. But even without our help, most animals can find something else to eat, though they may have to travel to find it.

That's one reason so many animals will be streaking across the road in lean acorn years. Wild turkeys come down out of the forested hills to forage in cornfields. Deer, in the midst of the rut, will have one more reason to roam, searching for twigs on which to browse. Chipmunks and squirrels forage farther afield. Although acorns are their usual staple, squirrels eat almost every kind of nut, seed, and fruit, and when those run out, they'll eat twigs and drink sap.

In city parks, gray squirrels have been known to nosh on everything from bagels to candy (they especially like the kinds with nuts). Red squirrels enjoy mushrooms. Ever wonder how those plucked mushrooms you sometimes see hanging, caps down, from the twigs or crotches of trees got there? Red squirrels brought them to dry before burying them under-ground.

Chipmunks' diets are eclectic, too. Although acorns are their favorite meal, they're not picky. In the summer, they'll even eat caterpillars, peeling away the prickly outsides like a person peels a banana to get to the green innards.

Even with their catholic tastes, rodents may still have a hard winter every now and then, especially when an acorn crop fails during a peak in rodent numbers. At Powdermill Biological Station in Rector, Pennsylvania, director Joseph Merritt has been studying small animals for more than two decades. Mild winters generally mean more rodents the following spring; and when rabies epidemics fell predators, even more baby rodents survive. But when an acorn crop fails on the heels of such events, that leaves loads of the little creatures scurrying about, looking for scarce food.

For bears, an acorn failure is particularly disruptive when it comes after earlier shortfalls. In 1995, for instance, a summer drought affected many of the foods black bears eat, including blueberries, huckleberries, blackberries, and beechnuts. Bears began to turn to garbage cans and dumps, campgrounds and cornfields and continued their raids into the fall. One ursine visitor broke through a western Massachusetts screen door and took some Milky Way bars off a kitchen table; there were several reports of bears stealing cooling pies off back porches. Then the acorn crop failed that fall. And the bears faced a further prob-lem: Having left the forested hills for suburban settings, they were easy targets for fall hunters. New Hampshire closed its hunting season early that year in response to the bears' dilemma, but in neighboring Massachusetts nearly twice as many bears as normal were killed by hunters.

Fortunately, bears can exercise an option in fall that many others cannot: they can go to bed early. In years of abundant nuts and mild temperature, many males may stay active all winter. (The females den to give birth.) But when there's little food available, bears can save energy simply by hibernating.

Blue jays cope in a different way. A dramatic indication of an acorn shortage is a mass exodus of blue jays. In abundant mast years, most jays stick around northern states all winter; if there's not enough, they fly south. After the dry summer and mast failure of 1995, Petersen remembers, "thousands flocked, milling around, blowing around like leaves. Flying high in the sky, with that lazy shallow flight, made it very hard to count them. But that was one big jay flight."

Not all left, of course. The birds are so resourceful that some of them always stick around, regardless of the lean pickings, and may resort to unusual menus. Stella Luster spotted a blue jay in the yard of the home where she works in Hancock, New Hampshire. The bird was eating cat food left out for a stray cat.

It was, however, the jay's last meal.

"I never thought anything could grab a bird that fast!" Luster said shortly after she saw the black stray appear from out of nowhere and snatch the hungry thief in its mouth.

How Migrating Birds
Change Their Lives

⅜

*W*e think we know songbirds. After all, many of them nest in our back yards. Vireos, warblers, and thrushes eat the insects that trouble us and enliven our summers with their songs.

But then comes fall, and the birds so familiar in summer turn mysterious.

Relatively few ornithologists have studied migrating songbirds. These tiny travellers fly at night, calling to one another to stay together in the darkness. It's nearly impossible to follow an individual. Unlike big birds such as geese, who can be outfitted with radio "backpacks" to transmit their location, songbirds are too small to carry telemetry equipment.

What little scientists have learned about migrating songbirds has only added to the mystery. Songbirds don't follow clearly defined "flyways" like ducks and geese do. Neither do the same individuals seem to regularly land at traditional stopovers. Even stranger, parent songbirds seem to fly south along a broad inland route; their young tend to follow the coast. Eighty to 95 percent of the songbirds you'll find along the Northeast coast in the fall are youngsters, many born only a month or two before—a tender age to take on a migration that can stretch for three thousand miles.

Flying at the height of hurricane season, these tiny singers alight on land they have never before seen. While a river of song-bird-eating hawks migrates overhead, the little birds must try to find enough food of their own to refuel for their next flight.

How do they do it? A former Brown University researcher may have found the answer among the scrubby thickets of Block Island.

Jeffrey Parrish first visited the island as he began the investi-gation that would lead to a Ph.D. from Brown University. "What struck me first," he says, "was the amazing amount of fruit." The same scene meets the eye of anyone who visits any Northeast coastal island, from the Isles of Shoals to Long Island. In practically every spot people haven't paved or covered with buildings, shrubs and vines fairly droop with fruit. You'll find bayberry, chokecherry, pokeweed, arrowwood, even poison ivy laden with juicy berries—and laced with songbirds plucking them with eager beaks.

But wait: what's wrong with this picture?

Songbirds are supposed to eat insects.

"Based on our knowledge of them in the breeding season, we've always thought of them as insectivores," says Parrish, "but it's basically not true. It depends on when you look at them."

And when you look at them in fall, at least along New England's coast, insect-eaters they aren't.

"Many of our migrating songbirds change their persona in the fall," says Massachusetts Audubon's field ornithologist Wayne Petersen. Take the eastern kingbird: By the end of sum-mer, this solitary, pugnacious flycatcher changes into a gregarious flocking species that chows down on fruit like a cedar waxwing. Even the familiar robin undergoes a Jeckyll and Hyde switch: come fall, the worm-eating redbreasts flock to Florida and ter-rorize orchardists with their newfound appetite for fruit.

If you watch the songbirds migrating through southern New England in the fall, you'll be surprised. Yellow-rumped warblers, swamp sparrows, hermit thrushes, gray catbirds, even the tree swallows who swoop after mosquitoes all summer long are busy eating berries. Most fall bird watchers have seen songbirds eat berries, but until Parrish's study, no one realized how crucial fruits are to these migrants.

To find out, Parrish's team watched the songbirds forage; they captured seven thousand birds of sixty-nine species in mist nets; and, last but not least, "invented the bird toilet."

Captured birds were detained in sock-like vessels with wire floors and plastic-bag basements. The nervous birds soon provided the researchers with droppings. Analysis of these yielded a surprise: for most migrants, fruit supplied more than half the diet. For hermit, Swainson's, and grey-cheeked thrushes, veeries, red-eyed vireos, and yellow-rumped warblers—all dedicated insect-eaters in the summer—fruit comprised 65 to 80 percent of their fall food.

But can birds fuel their marathon migration by fruit alone? In summer, when the going gets tough (and there's not much in this world that's tougher than having a nestful of mouths screaming at you for food every time you land), songbirds eat bugs. Bugs and worms are full of fat and protein—no wonder they're the Gerber of the nestling set.

Come fall, though, bugs and worms are less abundant, especially after first frost. Those that are left—midges, moths, flies—are scattered unpredictably. Unlike fruit, bugs can fly away and hide. And chasing them down is dangerous. The warbler flitting after a midge can make a fine meal for a migrating raptor; but the perch potato who gorges on bayberries can rest safely concealed in shiny foliage while he eats.

Still, compared to bugs, berries offer few calories. ("Remember the grapefruit diet?" Parrish recalls.) It seemed impossible that fruits could meet the extraordinary energy demands of migration.

Yet Parrish was astonished to find the fruit-eating migrants plump and healthy—some covered in fat from chin to belly.

How could this be? Parrish tried an experiment. He offered some of the captured songbirds a diet of nothing but wild fruits. He offered another group unlimited meal worms. And a third group could eat both. When the risks and bother of hunting for their food were removed, the birds who ate nothing but high fat, protein-rich worms, not surprisingly, gained more weight than those who ate fruit alone.

But the important finding was this: the birds who ate both fruit and worms gained the most weight of all—even more than those who ate only insects. His findings were published in the respected European ecological journal *Oecologia* and in the American ornithological journal *The Condor*.

Parrish, who is now a diplomacy fellow with the American Association for the Advance of Science, suspects that autumn triggers some metabolic change in migrating songbirds, allowing them to better assimilate the nutrients in fruits. Berries may not be merely last-ditch emergency rations. They may well be the best choice for the job ahead.

And the same could prove true for the routes the young birds take. For many years, ornithologists assumed that these naive navigators ended up along the coast by mistake, haplessly blown by northwest winds. As Parrish's studies suggest, "there may be more to it than that," says Petersen. "They may be there not by happenstance, but by design."

Then, what are the older birds doing inland? That's a study no one's done yet.

Migrating North—To Stay

Birds Expand Their Ranges

༄

*I*ts bright flash of crimson is a tonic to enliven the bleakest of days. But north of Boston (where folks could arguably use the cheer most) a winter visit from a cardinal—the only red bird with a crest—was once a rare event. Northern New Englanders could only envy Connecticut for its cardinals, its pert tufted titmice, and the often comical lyrics of its mockingbirds—all "southern" birds most Yankees seldom heard or saw.

Until about fifteen years ago. Today, feeders, woods, and waterways throughout northern New England are alive with birds historically abundant south of the Mason-Dixon line. Cardinals, after all, are known as "Virginia red birds" and "Kentucky cardinals." The Carolina wren sounds out of place breeding in southern Vermont and New Hampshire, as does the "Louisiana heron" wading in Massachusetts marshes (now they call it the tricolored heron). But, says Massachusetts Audubon ornithologist Wayne Petersen, they're part of "a big picture: there's a decided trend for southern birds to move north."

Some of the newcomers, like the titmouse and red-bellied woodpecker, can now be seen year-round; others, like the Acadian flycatcher, blue-winged and cerulean warbler, snowy egret, and turkey vulture, are migrants who come farther north each year to nest in the spring and summer.

For northern birders, the news seems almost too good to be

true. Just in the last two years, Ray David, producer of Bird-watch America trade shows for the bird-watching trade, has noticed titmice flocking to the seed and suet smorgasbord he lays out behind his rural Hancock home in southern New Hampshire. But even he is loathe to believe his own eyes. "Is it the birds moving north, or is it that more people are watching and noticing birds?" he wonders.

The northward trend is real, assures Kenneth V. Rosenberg. As a research associate in bird population studies at Cornell's Laboratory of Ornithology in Ithaca, New York, he's been gathering data on the question for ten years. Observations collected through the Lab's FeederWatch, a nationwide citizen research initiative, also shows that a few species are spreading their range south. The tiny, olive-colored golden-crowned kinglet and the red-breasted nuthatch, both birds of northern spruce forests, are now breeding as far south as New Jersey, where foresters began planting Norway spruce and Scotch pine fifty years ago.

But the overall trend among American bird species, he confirms, is a clear shift northward—with even more species headed this way.

Most folks are delighted with the pioneers. A few are worried. And everyone's intrigued. What's bringing them here? No one answer seems to explain it all.

Petersen points out that for a few species, bird feeders may be the attraction. "Food is the limiting factor for birds, not cold," he explains. According to a 1991 survey by the U.S. Fish and Wildlife Service, as many as 63 million Americans now offer seed, suet, and fruit in back yard feeders. Some species, like the seed-loving cardinal, may be able to afford to expand their ranges into areas they once shunned, simply because now they can find enough to eat.

But feeders don't explain the whole picture, because many of the expanding species don't eat seeds or frequent back yards. When a slew of southern egrets and herons began nesting in Massachusetts in the 1970s, Petersen knew there must be some other explanation—though he still isn't sure what it is.

He was surprised to discover, in 1974 on Clark's Island in

Plymouth, the first recorded Massachusetts nest of the glossy ibis—a green and brown marsh bird with a sickle-shaped bill that, as recently as 1920, was known to nest only in central Florida. But many more new wading species were found nesting during the Massachusetts Breeding Bird Atlas project from 1974–1979. They included the tricolored heron and the cattle egret—an African species that spread to Florida in the 1950s via South America. The survey also noted other waders, previously only occasional nesters, increasing in number. Today, Massachusetts' coastal islands host hundreds of snowy egrets, dozens of great egrets, and about twenty little blue herons. And within this same time period, egrets began to nest regularly on the Isles of Shoals, in southern Maine, and along coastal Connecticut and Rhode Island. A drought in these species' southwestern nesting grounds, Petersen theorizes, might have propelled them north—where they now return to nest every year.

New England's regrowing forests, as dense woods reclaim farmlands, may have made the north more attractive to still other species. The tufted titmouse, for instance, frequents feeders but favors deciduous forests with tall trees. Red-bellied woodpeckers were rare vagrants to southern New England in the 1950s, but now regularly winter and nest here.

Yet many scientists worry that another, more sweeping and more insidious change may also be at work: global warming. Environmental scholar, author, and syndicated columnist Donella Meadows was among the first to pose the idea that bird populations could be reflecting actual changes in climatic zones. For while southern birds are pushing their ranges north, some northern birds—like the Swainson's thrush, olive-sided flycatcher, and Bicknell's thrush—seem to be getting pushed off the map.

"These changes are subtle and complex, and we may never know all the answers," says Rosenberg. But in at least once instance, the cause is refreshingly clear. The northern incursion of the house finch, for instance, was a clear-cut case of what could be called "liberation ornithology."

In his encyclopedic book *Lives of North American Birds*,

sponsored by the Roger Tory Peterson Institute, Tucson-based ornithologist Kenn Kaufman explains what happened. Native to the American West, rose-colored house finches were once illegally sold in New York pet shops as "Hollywood finches." But when shop owners got word of a federal raid in the 1940s, they simply let the birds loose. The adaptable finches soon colonized New York suburbs and advanced both north and west. Now they're not only common at New England feeders, but soon destined to meet their western kin as a result of their continuing expansion.

A species most of us have never seen may soon be among our most familiar back yard birds. One Kaufman predicts is coming soon: the Eurasian collared dove—a middle-eastern native that has inexplicably began to expand its range from Turkey in 1910 through Europe and by 1970, had colonized England on up through Iceland. Fortunately, Kaufman says, this attractive buff bird with pink feet doesn't seem to be making trouble for native birds.

Accidentally introduced to the Bahamas in 1974, it spread to Florida, and now has reached as far as Texas and Tennessee— with no sign of stopping. They're coming to a feeder near you soon: Kaufman predicts they'll hit New England by 2010.

Bucks in Love

ॐ

On a November morning in a forest near Manchester, Vermont, Peter Pekins crouched, transfixed, as three deer approached him to within thirty yards. A doe led the way, followed by two bucks—a big male whose antlers bore six or eight tines, and a young "spiker" whose antlers were mere points. The doe was ready to mate, which the bucks well knew from her scent. Both had the same idea in mind.

The two bucks squared off to fight for the privilege of mating the doe. As the contested female watched from the side, the bucks lowered their heads and locked antlers. For perhaps fifteen seconds—though it seemed much longer—they pushed against each other, hair bristling, thick necks bulging with strain. And then, to Pekins' amazement, the larger male picked up the spikehorn on his antlers and flipped him backwards, head over heels.

That was Pekins' first hunting season, more than twenty years ago. "I sat there in awe, instead of bagging my first buck," he said. After the spikehorn ran off, finally it occurred to him to shoot—but he fired too late. Pekins thought he knew where the remaining pair might go, and raced upslope, expecting a long run. But he came upon them only thirty-five yards away. "I was in shock," he said. "There was the buck, mounted on the doe. And these animals had just been shot at by a high-powered rifle."

He's glad his shot missed. The drama that he witnessed, thanks to that missed shot, has nourished his understanding of these magnificent creatures for two decades—far longer than he would have enjoyed the venison in the freezer. What he saw, says Pekins, now a professor of wildlife management at the University of New Hampshire in Durham, "is the power of reproduction. And that is what drives the decisions of all the deer out there come fall."

The rut causes deer to alter their behavior. Normally shy and secretive creatures take astonishing risks—affording you an unrivaled opportunity to see them during some of the most dramatic moments of their lives. One November day, Don Schrock of Peterborough, New Hampshire, was driving on busy Route 2A in Lunenberg, past a meadow in which now sits a Wal-Mart. And there, right in the open, at 3 p.m., he saw a doe with a huge antlered buck behind her— "and another buck is right behind him, and another eight- to ten-point buck on a hill—and then a lesser buck started running toward them down the hill. It was like, 'Take a number,'" said Schrock, a skilled hunter who has spent hundreds of days in the woods stalking the elusive creatures. He pulled his truck off the road to watch. One of the larger bucks chased the smaller buck away, and then resumed his place in 'line.' "By the time we finally left, there were thirty cars pulled over to watch," he said. "Three police cars had to escort everyone away, it was creating such a traffic jam."

The rut transforms animals normally as placid as Bambi into gladiators. In his classic reference book, *The Deer of North America,* Leonard Lee Rue describes bucks in rut as "time bombs ready to explode at any moment." One tame buck, he reports, raised on a Michigan deer farm, attacked his owner and killed a doe and two bucks in two days.

"They go berserk, almost," says Pekins. At the university's Brentwood Wildlife Facility, where deer are kept in large pens for physiological studies, the deer eat out of his hands—until one day the rut descends upon a buck. "Now, he is going to kill you," Pekins says. "And it doesn't matter if yesterday he almost let you ride around on his back."

Though, in New England, the rut may begin as early as mid-October and last through January, the excitement reaches its peak in mid- to late November. Then, bucks are on the move 24 hours a day, restlessly searching out does.

It is a time of lust and battle, at the confluence of life's beginning and often, life's end. During the weeks in which most does conceive, more deer die than any other time of year—and not just due to hunting season. Half of all the deer killed by cars in Massachusetts die during the three weeks of November when the rut is at its height, says John McDonald, Deer Project leader at the state Division of Fisheries and Wildlife. Watch out for a doe springing across the street in front of your car at night, he warns—she's usually followed by a buck, with possibly a second buck in pursuit.

Those bucks have just one thing on their minds. In September, many weeks before the first does are ready to mate, newly adult males leave their families and older bucks leave their bachelor groups. Results of radio telemetry studies by the Massachusetts' Deer Project show they travel far more widely than previously thought. "We used to say deer don't move but one mile," said McDonald, "but some move two to five miles every two weeks." One young male radio-collared in Carlisle was shot last year thirty miles away in Topsfield—and to get there, he had successfully crossed Routes 3, 93, 95, and 1.

Few does are ready to mate before November. The bucks take out their frustrations on saplings, brush, and earth. They bash bushes and trees with their antlers. They rub secretions from glands in the forehead on branches. The largest bucks also rake the earth with their hooves, advertising their status. In the woods you might encounter their "scrapes," circular patches of earth three feet across and several inches deep churned among the leaves, usually adorned with pellet-like feces and smelling of their acrid urine. If you find a scrape, look above it: you may see the branches of a bush or low-growing tree four or five feet above the ground scored by his antlers.

Meanwhile, the does are occupied with sensible concerns, such as eating. Surprisingly, deer eat a lot of fallen leaves—up to ten thousand a day. According to Rue, deer particularly relish dogwoods and the red leaves of maples, with their high sugar content. Deer love acorns (which comprise up to 80 percent of the fall diet in some areas), and particularly relish the sweet nuts of the white oak, as well as beechnuts and apples. Especially at dawn, dusk, and dark, a good place to find deer in autumn is beneath one of these trees. (It's also a good bet a hunter may be nearby, so wear orange. It'll alert hunters, but not deer. Deer can't see orange—but they can see blue, advises McDonald, so "don't wear blue jeans unless you want to stick out like a sore thumb.")

Bucks know to look for does here, so be careful: though deer are usually gentle creatures, in the rut, the 200-plus pound males can attack both men and women (especially menstruating women, whose odors apparently remind bucks of receptive does). If a buck flattens his ears and stares hard at you, he considers you a rival. Be prepared to climb a tree.

If there's an adult doe nearby, chances are the buck's attention is focused on her. You might see him curl his lip in a gesture called flehmen, testing the air with a special organ in the roof of the mouth for chemical cues to test whether she is ready to conceive. If she's not, she will run away from him. But if she is, and consents to his attentions, the couple may caress each other for several minutes, running their tongues over each other's head and back and rubbing their bodies together before they mate. Since a doe may be receptive for only one day, the buck may stay near her throughout this period, guarding her from other bucks.

Often a snort and show of antlers is enough to ward off an interloper. Most bucks know the other bucks in the area, and dominance has already been established. But sometimes, the meeting of two strange bachelors is occasion for a dramatic battle:

"While circling or approaching each other, the bucks tuck their chins in so that their antlers are tilted forward," Rue writes. "With their ears flattened against their necks and pointing to the rear, and with the whites of their eyes showing, the bucks look 'mean as hell,' and they are ... The erect hair and the bunched muscles make a buck appear a picture of powerful, controlled fury."

The two bucks may be twenty feet apart when they finally lunge. They hit with explosive impact: one observer witnessed an antler break off and fly twenty feet into the air.

The antlers, though, are not used as weapons. "The fight is a pushing match," says Pekins. The antlers, as well as showcasing its owner's strength (older, healthier bucks have larger racks), serve to engage and lock the pushing match between two bucks.

Sometimes—though rarely—the antlers lock so well they can't come apart, dooming both combatants to death from exhaustion and thirst. In North Dakota, one struggling pair of bucks apparently attracted a third buck. All three were later discovered in the woods dead, their antlers locked together—a sculptural testament to the magnificence and the madness of the rut.

Mammals on the Move

Biologists were perplexed. The two rabbit species looked nearly identical, and seemed to inhabit identical habitats. But one—the eastern cottontail, an introduced interloper—was pushing out the native species, the New England cottontail. No one knew why.

That's the question that Gus Smith tackled for his Ph.D. thesis at the University of New Hampshire in Durham. The answer, he was to find, lay not in the brushy fields overgrown with multiflora rose, dogwood saplings, and autumn olive where both species lived—but in the differing ways the two kinds of rabbits saw the landscape.

What does a given landscape look like to a non-human mammal? "It may look very different from the picture humans see," says Thomas Kunz, director of Boston University's Program in Ecology and Conservation and president elect of the American Society of Mammalogists. The same roads that permit us to travel may be impassable barriers to other species. What looks to us like a rich woodland might seem, to a different mammal, a barren wasteland with nothing to eat—or a minefield of dangerous predators.

But by studying mammals' movements, researchers are now beginning to discover a whole new way of seeing the landscape—though another species' eyes.

"Movement serves as a link between organisms and the

environment around them," notes Patrick Zollner, a research ecologist with the U.S. Forest Service's North Central Research Station in Rhinelander, Wisconsin.

"What are the characteristics that drive animals to move? What are the expectations they have of the land around them? What do animals know and how are they making decisions about the landscape? These are the questions we have to ask," he says.

When a young adult chipmunk or pine martin or sea lion strikes out to find new territory, he points out, "it's like Odysseus striking out over the Agean Sea—these are vast Homerian movements."

"We are now starting to collect very different kinds of data—both fine scale and large scale," he says. "We are going to be able to move beyond merely observing patterns, and get to an understanding of the mechanisms animals are actually using to respond to the landscape."

Take the New England and eastern cottontails. To find out how the two species perceive the landscape, Smith captured a number of cottontails of both species and confined each to a large outdoor pen in an overgrown field. He then placed bowls of rabbit chow at various distances from the thickest cover in the pen. How far would each species venture from the most overgrown areas to get to the chow? Their movements would show how safe each considered the same landscape and reflect how each would use the same land.

His results: the New England cottontails wouldn't venture farther than three meters beyond cover. They saw the three meters beyond the thickest cover as a small, safe haven beyond which the risks of being caught by a predator outweighed the benefits of the extra meals. But the eastern cottontails—a more southern species hunters introduced to New England in the 1930s—traveled twenty meters beyond cover to get the food. To this species, the whole pen looked like a safe home.

That's why the relatively fearless eastern cottontail has spread so far, so fast, at the expense of the native species. "You've got this Superbunny, and then this other rabbit adapted to dense cover that isn't there anymore," Smith says. New England cottontails prefer fields that have been abandoned for ten to fifteen years, offering very dense cover. But eastern cottontails—perhaps because their eyes bulge out slightly farther than the native species, offering a better view of approaching foxes, owls, and coyotes, he suggests—can colonize fields only seven years after they have been abandoned. By the time a field grows up to the type of cover New England cottontails prefer, "guess who's already there?"

Today, because of human development, abandoned fields are at a premium. Humans have also changed the predator mix: the wolves and cougars (to which the New England species may have been better adapted) were killed off in the last century by bounty hunters; in their place are more red foxes and coyotes, predators who flourish in today's increasingly suburbanized landscape.

Human activity has profoundly changed animal movements in ways scientists are only now beginning to explore. "The movement of animals through a fragmented landscape will become one of the main issues in conservation biology in the future," asserts Harry P. Andreassen, a University of Oslo researcher studying the movements of root voles in Oslo, Norway.

The spatial arrangement of managed forest stands and conifer swamps might be the reason that American martens aren't spreading through the Nicolet and Chequamegon National Forests in Northern Wisconsin as fast as wildlife managers had expected. These handsome, tree-dwelling weasels were trapped out of the state in the 1920s for their valuable fur; wildlife managers began reintroducing them in the 1980s. And although winter snow-tracking surveys show the population is healthy, the animals haven't spread as far or as fast as predicted. Eric Gustafson, a research ecologist with the U.S. Forest Service's North Central Research Station is using a computer model—a "virtual marten"—to try to find out why.

American martens, like many other animals, strike out in young adulthood to find new territories—this is how a species avoids inbreeding and expands it range. From trappers who have reported catching martens scientists have marked with ear tags, researchers know that young martens can travel up to one hundred miles from where they were born. But "the details of dispersal are poorly known," says Gustafson. "And it's a critical event for the health of a population. It's very difficult to observe."

How do the young American martens decide where to go? What are the barriers they face on their journey? How are they choosing their route through the landscape?

To find out, Gustafson programmed his "virtual marten" into a computer. At any given point on a grid-based map, the virtual critter is faced with the risks and benefits of moving into any of the eight "cells" around it. Where will it go? The virtual marten, though unreal, is no fool: it tends to choose cells with more prey and less risk of being eaten itself. "We simulate ten thousand of these critters at a time," Gustafson says. "Looking at their combined travel routes, the corridors and barriers emerge. That's how you can get a sense of what they're up against."

From the computer simulations, Gustafson suspects the dispersing martens might be flummoxed by areas of forest with little slash—areas with few broken branches and downed trees. Slash creates excellent habitat for creatures like shrews, which martens depend upon for food. "It might suggest portions of the landscape can't meet [the American martens'] energy requirements," he said. "They might be encountering a wasteland they can't cross. It doesn't look like a wasteland to us, but if it doesn't have enough shrews and voles to eat, it would limit their expansion."

If the computer model works, potentially one could program the features of any park or forest into a computer and discover whether the landscape is appropriate for conserving or reintroducing the animal—and it could potentially be modified for other animals too.

To test the computer model, the forestry team is working with engineers to design lighter, better telemetry for martens. Radio telemetry, which has been used on animals since the 1960s, doesn't convey the detail researchers need. Relying on VHF signals from a radio transmitter worn on the animals' back requires several people to follow the animal with receivers, and can only yield one or two locations a day—provided the animal is in range and the signal doesn't bounce off trees or rocks, misleading the trackers. The goal is to outfit the marten with a super-miniaturized computer, worn like a backpack, that would communicate with a satellite to convey the marten's position every thirty to sixty minutes for nine months.

Because the device needs to be light enough for a small mammal to carry, that goal may be a few years away yet for martens. But it's already a reality for southern elephant seals. A revolution in remote sensing technology is already making it possible for scientists to see the underwater pathways that marine mammals like seals and whales use on their mysterious peregrinations.

At Gatty Marine Laboratory at the University of St. Andrews in Scotland, biologists and engineers have devised signaling and recording devices they glue onto the backs of elephant seals to track, with astonishing accuracy, the one- to three-ton creatures' routes in three dimensions though the uncharted seas.

"The system allows us to see underwater," says Bernie Mc-Connell of the Sea Mammal Research Unit at St. Andrews. Developed to work with the French polar-orbiting satellite system ARGOS, the fist-sized devices record the animals' position two or three times daily. Wildlife researchers have used such systems, originally developed for weather information, for more than a decade, but new miniaturized computers now make it possible for the animal-borne transmitters to convey information in far greater detail. The St. Andrews unit also contains a dive computer to monitor depth, speed, and other characteristics. The computer inside stores the information and then, when the animal surfaces to breathe, beams it to an overhead satellite that then feeds the information into the Gatty scientists' computers in Scotland. "This gives us a huge new window into how the animals behave at sea," McConnell said.

The system already has allowed researchers to begin solving one of the great mysteries of these submarine creatures. Half the world's population of 600,000 elephant seals are born on South Georgia Island in the Southern Atlantic. Gaining four times their birthweight in three weeks, the suckling pups suddenly face an astonishing hurdle: once they're weaned, all the adults leave the island. The babies, just learning to swim, must somehow find their way to feeding grounds, rich in squid and fish, in the sea five hundred to one thousand kilometers away. How do they do it? Where do they go?

Data from dozens of baby elephant seals suggest that a number of them are taking the same route: a thousand-mile arc east and south, towards Antarctica. But they don't all travel at the same time. Some take the same route many days apart. Others arrive at the same location by different routes. The data suggests the seals may possess unknown navigational abilities, or that they are able to communicate with each other or with adult seals underwater to follow the same undersea pathways.

But today's new studies of animal movement don't always rely on high-tech gizmos. Forest Ecologist Zollner's studies yield detailed information about how small creatures such as squirrels see the landscape—with spools of thread.

Zollner was investigating a question similar to Gustafson's: how do animals find appropriate habitat? Specifically, from how far away could they detect the woodlands they needed? To find out, he captured fox squirrels, gray squirrels, and chipmunks in remote woodlots of West Central Indiana and Illinois and transported them to barren agricultural fields bordered on only one side with suitable forest.

Before releasing the animals, he attached to each one's back a spool of thread, one end of which was tied to the release mechanism. The animals were then released at varying distances from the woods. As each animal left the mechanism, it left a trail of thread, like Hansel and Gretel's breadcrumbs, that showed the exact route the animal took. A straight line to the woods would show that the animal had a good idea where the forest was.

Zollner found that each species had a different "perceptual range": fox squirrels made a beeline for woodlands from 400 meters away. Gray squirrels could find woodlands 300 meters away. And chipmunks could only find woodlands that were within 120 meters of their release site.

The data is important because it shows why some species may be absent from isolated woodlots: even if these woodlots contain appropriate habitat, an animal can't colonize it if it doesn't know it's there. And as roads, homes, and cities break up forests and fields into smaller and smaller islands, an animals' perceptual range may figure importantly into conservation plans.

But then Zollner came up against a conundrum. A colleague, working with conventional radio telemetry, was reporting completely different results in a neighboring area. Tracking the squirrels with VHF radio telemetry, he found his gray squirrels were easily travelling to a new woodlot, nearly a mile away! "This was way beyond anything my data showed they could perceive," says Zollner.

By combining their data sets in a computer simulation, the researchers figured out what was happening. A telephone wire across the agricultural fields linked the two forest patches—unwittingly opening up new territory for squirrels the way the railroads opened the western United States for people.

Tracking the Vanished Glacier

༰

*O*n a brilliant autumn afternoon, David Roberts has gone to
the cemetery to read the testimony of the stones.

At St. Mary's Cemetery in Wellesley, Massachusetts, he ig-
nores the inscriptions on the tombstones. Roberts has come to
read a much older story—one written on an elephant-size chunk
of bedrock protruding from the ground atop which three cement
angels are perched.

"Look," he says, pointing to the dark, parallel gouges running over the top of the rock. "They're all going the same way.
And here," he says, stroking another spot, where the rock is naturally polished, "feel how smooth!"

Former geology teacher, petroleum geologist, and author of
the Peterson Field Guides' *Geology of Eastern North America*,
Roberts reads the textures of rocks the way a palmist reads lines
on a hand. "Rocks are just sitting there ready to talk to you," he
says. "Practically every rock has something to tell you, if you only
know what to look for. You can get a lot of soul-satisfaction from
speculating on the past."

Here in a cemetery built in 1881, the past he sees stretches
back more than two million years. Among the graves memorial-
izing fifteen thousand brief human lives, the outcrop testifies to a
vanished force that dominated this part of our continent for
eons—a force that changed the northeast landscape and profoundly affected the lives of the people buried here.

On this autumn day on the cusp of winter, Roberts reads the story of the Ice Age. For much of two million years, glaciers up to a mile thick covered much of the Northeast, the ice so heavy it weighted down the bedrock, which is still readjusting itself today.

Parallel gouges in the outcrop here trace the southward path of these immense Ice Age glaciers, as pebbles and boulders imbedded at the bottom of the ice clawed at the bedrock and smaller stones and sand polished the bedrock smooth.

"Today, hardly a place in the Northeast does not show the shaping influence of ice," Chet and Maureen Raymo write in their book, *Written in Stone: A Geological History of the United States*. In fact, some of New England's most famous landmarks were sculpted by glaciers: Plymouth Rock was plucked and transported to the spot where the Pilgrims landed by a conveyor belt of flowing ice. Bunker Hill, Dorchester Heights, and the Boston Harbor islands are glacial drumlins, masses of clay and gravel gathered and dumped by the ice. Many of New England's ponds, including Thoreau's beloved Walden, and many of our sinuous, winding ridges, are also the handiwork of melting ice sheets.

"The glaciers have affected nature, and our history, and the way in which we use the land," says Richard Moore, a geologist with the U.S. Geological Survey. He notes that the bricks for the settlers' chimneys were made from the clays deposited in glacial lakes; these same clays supplied the bricks for the mills of Lowell, Massachusetts and Manchester, New Hampshire. The pines from which settlers built their homes grew on the sandy soils left behind by the glaciers.

To see the evidence of the vanished ice sheets, you need not travel far—but you must read subtle, and sometimes counter-intuitive clues. Even pebbles can tell a great story. Just a mile from his son's home in Wellesley, Roberts visits a gravel pit near the local swimming hole. Climbing halfway up the slope of the pit, he points out the surface is strewn with large pebbles, some as big as softballs, among the sand and gravel. "Look at the rocks here," he points out, his blue eyes twinkling beneath a denim cap. Within the space of a square foot, he picks up a red sand-stone, a gray crystalline metamorphic rock, pink quartz, white sandstone. "They're not local," he explains. "How did these pebbles get here?"

"The only thing that could bring them," he continues, "is running water—with a pretty stiff current, strong enough to wash the little stuff away." But where's the water? The swimming hole is far below us, at a lower level than the gravel pit. So where did that current come from?"

Roberts pauses for a teacher's dramatic effect.

"A melting glacier in the Ice Age."

Even during the Ice Age, temperatures warmed enough for glaciers to start melting. Four different times over the last 2.3 million years, the climate of the northern hemisphere changed enough to support giant glaciers that grew and joined with huge ice fields that were already in the mountain ranges—and then melted away again.

When the ice advanced, it pushed everything in front of it like a bulldozer. Moving ice can carry more and larger rocks than water can, so boulders (like Plymouth Rock, and the much larger Bartlett Boulder and Sawyer Rock near Bartlett Station, New Hampshire) were dropped by the glacier itself rather than by its meltwater rivers.

Each time the glacier melted, it revealed a changed landscape. To see more glacial handiwork, just a few miles from the gravel pit, we stop by a willow-fringed pond where mallards and Canada geese paddle. Roberts begins to climb the ridge overlooking it.

The ridge is as steeply pitched as a tent, and as sinuous as a river. And, in fact, Roberts explains, this ridge is the remains of a river—the gravel bed of a river that ran on, inside, or under the glacial ice.

The river carved stream-tunnels in the ice, which collected gravel and cobbles. When the glacier melted, the gravel remained, creating this esker. "The river was as wide as the base of this ridge," Roberts explains. "Where the riverbed was thickest, the esker is highest." So the melting of the glacier transformed what was once a river to a ridge. Geologists are able to trace river systems in the ice by mapping the eskers, making visible a force that melted away ten thousand years ago.

If you look back, beyond today's ridge, millions of years into the past, you can see an extinct river; and if you look back beyond the graves at St. Mary's Cemetery, you can see where a chunk of glacial ice was buried.

The angels on the outcrop gaze in the direction of a kitchen-size depression, marked with a small boulder at its bottom. This is another mark of the glacier, explains Roberts: it's known as a kettle hole. Here, at one edge of a glacier, as the ice melted back, a block of ice remained behind. Sand and gravel flushed by melt-water streams from the glacier buried the ice block. And when the ice block finally melted, it left this depression.

This is how so many of New England's ponds were formed; graves for melting chunks of glaciers.

How Blue Jays Replanted Northern Oak Forests

ॐ

*T*he ice once stretched all the way from the Arctic to Pennsylvania, from Washington State across to New Jersey. During the Pleistocene, winter was very long: it lasted most of two million years.

But spring came fast on the heels of the glacier. In fact, oak and beech forests returned to the north far more rapidly than anyone could explain. Once the glacier retreated ten thousand years ago, studies of fossilized pollen show, the oaks were back within a thousand years. Beech returned nine thousand years ago. Geologists calculate the oaks advanced north at the lively rate of 380 yards a year. Not bad for an organism that's rooted to the ground.

Of course, trees don't get up and move—but their seeds do. The whirligigs of ash and maple and the feather-light seeds of spruce travel fast as the wind. But oaks beat spruce to New England by a millennium. How did the big, heavy acorns and beechnuts move north so quickly?

"This was the classic puzzle for paleoecology for years," says Thompson Webb III, a geologist at Brown University. "How did the north get re-vegetated? How did you get the seeds of those heavy nuts going at the rate they were moving?"

Squirrels, though industrious, can't take credit. They bury

nuts only a few dozen yards from where they find them. Wild ducks and turkeys eat acorns and beechnuts, but these seeds never grow because they're destroyed in the birds' gizzards.

W. Carter Johnson, a biology professor at Virginia Polytechnic Institute, was contemplating this mystery while eating his lunch one day beneath an oak tree. And then, like Newton's apple, the answer hit him. A shower of acorn shells fell on his head. He looked up to see a family of blue jays.

Holding the nut in place on the branch with the feet, hammering the shell with the lower jaw, they'd cracked open the shells that fell on the professor's head. But jays don't eat most of the seeds they find in fall, as Johnson knew. As he watched the birds fly off with acorns in their beaks, he realized they might lead him, with Webb, to solve one of the great mysteries of paleoecology and to a whole new understanding of the process by which bare land transforms into woods.

"Everyone recognizes the blue jay—one of the most common birds in the U.S.," he says, "but no studies had been done to recognize its significance in the ecosystem."

How important are these noisy, showy birds to our landscape? "They're essential," says Johnson. Blue jays, it now appears, replanted almost all of the north's oak and beech forest.

And in the wake of 20th-century bulldozers, they're at it again. Jays may well be the link connecting fragmented forests, carrying the seeds of beech, oak, and chestnuts across highways or towns no squirrel would dare cross. And because of jays, these trees may be among the earliest to colonize young forests— rather than the latecomers most ecologists have always thought them to be. Studies of blue jays have helped foresters understand the forest's past—and future—in a new way. "All of a sudden," says Dave Houston, recently retired from the Agriculture Department's Center for Forest Health Research in Hamden, Connecticut, "it opened up what we had suspected but not known: That something was moving these seeds around."

You can watch jays at work outside your window. Some blue jays migrate—in lean years, more than others—but some always stick around. Those who plan to stay spend much of fall salting away food for the winter. With ornithologist Curtis Adkisson, Johnson found marked jays in Wisconsin regularly made round-trip flights of up to five miles from food trees to the territories where they'd store the food to dig up later.

Blessed with an expandable esophagus, a single blue jay can fit as many as three white oak acorns, five pin oak acorns, or fourteen beechnuts in its throat at a time—a load a tenth of its own body weight. And then, to make the most of each flight, the bird often collects one last nut in the bill before flying back to its territory. Watching birds marked with identifying leg bands at a Virginia study site, Johnson's student, Susan Darley-Hill, discovered that in 28 days, about 50 jays transported 150,000 acorns—58 percent of the total nut crop from 11 pin oaks.

Each bird takes more than it needs. But in this case, greed pays off for everyone: the buried nuts not only feed jays through the winter, but also provision small mammals and ensure future forests.

With its beak, the jay shoves the nut into soft soil or short grass. The bird camouflages each cache carefully, covering it over with plant debris. If no one digs it up, it's planted as surely as if a gardener did it.

And jays are remarkably efficient gardeners. When Johnson and Adkisson collected the beechnuts the birds had picked and germinated them in a greenhouse, 88 percent of the sample grew—compared with only 10 percent of those the researchers plucked at random. (Studies of crows and nutcrackers, which are closely related to jays, show these birds test seeds for soundness by rattling them in their bills; they dump the rejects.) And although jays hide seeds almost anywhere—creek banks, post holes, the forest floor—most often, Johnson reported, they plant them in open land at the edge of shrubs or woods. Exactly the right place for an oak to grow.

Of course, planting future forests is not what the jay has in mind. Jays dig up buried seeds all winter. Recent work suggests the birds even remember where they hid them. Working with Clark's nutcrackers, a related seed-caching bird, northern Arizona researcher Russ Balda found the birds always buried and retrieved pine seeds near objects like posts and branches decorating their sand-floored aviary. Was this the key to their system? To find out, the researcher rearranged the cage furnishings. The dismayed nutcrackers continued to search for seeds in the same positions they had hidden them, relative to the landmarks they remembered.

Jays might use similar "beacons" to recall where they hide seeds. And if so, this knowledge could explain much about the patterns in which certain trees grow.

Houston strongly suspects that for blue jays, those beacons may be a few tall pines.

Houston was working on a study of sugar maples in New York when something in an abandoned field nearby caught his eye. In the old field, where someone had planted pines forty years before, beech seedlings were growing—yet there were no mature beeches anywhere around. Where had the seeds come from? He found the nearest possible parent beech was downhill, up and over a ridge seven hundred feet away.

Intrigued, he took a closer look and saw another strange thing: the beech seedlings were all growing near pines or pine stumps, in a semicircular pattern. With his plant geneticist brother, he took tissue samples of the seedlings. They were all genetically related. Most of them had sprung from seeds of the same tree.

Only one thing could account for these patterns. Blue jays had been at work there.

Although retired from the forest service, Houston continues to investigate the role blue jays may have played in planting beeches. He is particularly interested in learning why some beeches are resistant to beech bark disease—a devastating fungus spread by sucking insects accidentally imported from England at the turn of the century. Resistant trees, he notes, typically grow in groups—groups that were almost certainly planted by blue jays.

Meanwhile, the jays continue their work, too. Like a squadron of avian Johnny Appleseeds, they're airlifting acorns, beechnuts, and chestnuts to the very places that need them most.

They're seeding red pine plantations with oaks, trees whose fruit will feed animals from bears to squirrels. They're establishing new forests at the edges of newly cleared suburbs. Johnson, now a professor at South Dakota State University, has even received reports that jays are replanting scrub oak amid abandoned orange groves in Florida.

"The blue jay is taking better care of the land near us than we are," says Johnson, "like a repair squad coming in after us."

Winter

Bird Irruptions

꙰

*H*ugh Wiberg stared out his back window on a January morning, dumbstruck: his Wilmington, Massachusetts back yard was covered with five-inch-long sparrowlike birds with red splotches on their heads and small black bibs.

Redpolls are arctic birds—with plumage so dense they can maintain a temperature 163° warmer than the outside air—who normally winter hundreds of miles north of us. Wiberg, who is president of the Tynsboro Birding Society and author of *Hand Feeding Wild Birds*, hadn't seen a single redpoll all winter—or the winter before. But that snowy day, his yard was "like a beehive of birds," he said. The redpolls were too many to count. He would get up to sixty or seventy, but with all the birds aflutter, he'd lose track. They stayed one-and-a-half hours, until they had cleaned out all the sunflower seeds in his feeders. "I've never seen anything like it," he said. "It was breathtaking, there were so many."

Sometimes a sudden surge of birds blankets an entire region. In the winter of 1993–1994, it was red-breasted nuthatches. These compact, short-tailed birds were everywhere in record number, walking down trees head-first in their typical foraging pattern through most the northeast and central U.S. and southern Canada. Christmas bird counts—national bird surveys run by the Audubon societies—from twenty-nine different Massachusetts locations totaled 4,750 red-breasted nuthatches—ten times the previous year's survey. In Quabbin Reservoir alone,

1,886 were seen on one day—more than four times the number of nuthatches seen all over the state in the previous year's Christmas count.

The next year, nuthatches were rarely seen—but the whole country was awash in northern shrikes. These predatory song-birds—sometimes called butcher birds for their gruesome habit of skewering rodents and other songbirds on barbed-wire fences and thorns—are infrequent visitors to New England; few people ever see one. But incredibly, that year 561 of these solitary, cold-loving birds were tallied on the New England Christmas bird count, with well over 3,000 of them counted across the continent.

What is going on here? Ornithologists call such events irrup-tions—irregular mass movements of birds, far beyond their usual winter range. Irruptions of birds are just as spectacular as what a volcano does (that's an eruption)—and although far less destruc-tive, just as unpredictable and mysterious.

"Most years, some bird species is irrupting somewhere," says Steve Mirick, a board member of the Audubon Society of New Hampshire and a regional compiler for the Christmas bird count.

Three years after Wiberg's experience, the redpolls were at it again. "They seemed to be exploding," said Allison Wells, director of public outreach at Cornell University's Laboratory of Ornithology in Ithaca, New York, which tracks these events through its Irruptive Bird Survey each year. She reported that her own back yard feeder was "just crawling" with redpolls— and that was the trend all over the Northeast.

Why redpolls one year and not the next? Such questions have puzzled and intrigued birders for centuries. We tend to think of migration as a miracle of clockwork regularity: an indi-vidual ovenbird, for instance, flies to the same streamside in Mexico each winter and returns to nest in the same patch of New England oak forest in spring.

But irruptive species are totally different. Whether they will migrate at all in a given year, where they will go, and how they will find it are all mysteries. Sparrowlike pine siskins banded on the east coast one winter may fly to British Columbia, Washing-ton, Idaho, or California. Common redpolls captured in Quebec have flown south to New England—as well as west to Alaska. One redpoll flew from Michigan's Upper Peninsula to eastern Russia, a journey of 4,500 miles.

What causes these mass movements in a given year? Hard winters aren't responsible. Little redpolls can survive at 60° below. White winged crossbills, who live in spruce and tamarack forests from Alaska to Newfoundland—where their peculiar crossed bills allow them to pry open spruce cones to get at the seeds—will actually breed in the winter when it's 35° below.

After decades of study, ornithologists have come up with important clues. First, the cast of characters for each irruption is typically drawn from two broad types of northern birds: those who rely on rodents for food (such as the saw-whet, snowy, short eared, and great gray owls, and the rough-legged hawk and northern shrike); and those who eat particular types of seeds (such as the redpoll, pine siskin, purple finch, evening grosbeak, pine grosbeak, red crossbill, white-winged crossbill, and red-breasted nuthatch).

"Food is certainly an important part of what drives irruptions," says the Laboratory of Ornithology's Wells. Irruptive species leave their normal wintering grounds en masse when their food supplies run low. For instance, crossbills are cone specialists; they respond to reductions in spruce and fir cones. Siskins and redpolls feed on catkins, and depend on the seeds of birches, alders, and willows. Predatory northern birds like snowy owls and shrikes depend on rodents like lemmings and voles.

All of these foods are only available in erratic supply. Lemmings are well-known for their wild population fluctuations; vole numbers, too, dramatically peak and crash. But few people realize that seed production is often a boom-or-bust affair as well: often every birch, fir, spruce, and tamarack across thousands of square miles will yield bountiful harvests of seed one year—and little or none the next.

But this is only part of the picture. As Petersen points out, other factors play important roles as well: one year there may be plenty of red-backed voles in northern Canada, but if they're all under cover of ice-crusted snow, the owls can't get to them. Or one year there may well be a shortage of spruce and fir cones—

183

but perhaps it will fall in a year when crossbill populations are low, so there will be enough for everyone. Alternatively, even a moderately generous seed production year may be a disaster for a bird population that happens to be at an all-time high.

Two or more such factors can be at work in one year. The last redpoll irruption in New England was also accompanied by an unusually high incursion of saw-whet owls. Few people ever see these "round-headed little gnomes" as birder and author Kenn Kaufmann calls them in his book, *Lives of North American Birds*. They tend to sit motionless in the tops of conifers. But that winter, lots of folks heard their rhythmic toots in the night, for they appeared in record numbers. Massachusetts Audubon's Trailside Museum-based owl expert Norm Smith banded more than three hundred saw whets that fall. His banding excursions included two nights in Marshfield, when he captured thirty-one of them one night and thirty-eight of them on another.

If many food sources fail at once, northern birds may stage a spectacular, multi-species "superflight." This is what happened in the winter of 1993–'94. The nuthatches were joined by huge flocks of south-flying Bohemian waxwings, pine grosbeaks, and common redpolls. For waxwings, it was their greatest and possibly most widespread New England invasion on record, Petersen asserts. The waxwings and redpolls irrupted throughout the northeast, but the grosbeaks were concentrated in western Massachusetts. Why? No one knows.

But this is the kind of question that ornithologists, with the help of back yard birders, are hoping to answer in coming years. The Laboratory of Ornithology's Backyard Bird Count, along with its Web-based Irruptive Bird Survey, is combining data from thousands of volunteer "citizen-scientists" on what birds appear where and when. This information will help assemble a better picture of the size and scope of any given irruption, and how food availability affects where the birds go and how long they stay.

Meanwhile, irruptions keep birders glued to their windows and binoculars. "If we had the same things every winter, birding would become a boring pastime," says Mirick. "That's part of the excitement of birding that turns me on."

Yikes! ... Shrikes!

࿓

*F*or most of his life, Hugh Wiberg has begun each winter weekend by stoking up the bird feeders in his Wilmington back yard. His kids—and now his grandkids—watch birds like most kids watch television.

One morning twenty-five years ago, though, Wiberg was left wondering if his little daughter would have been better off watching cartoons.

His daughter, Wendy, was ten then, but she still remembers the scene. She was standing by the window, watching the birds enjoy their feast—until, as the elder Wiberg recalls, "a gray rocket came in from the right."

The rocket shot towards the thistle feeder, knocking a finch to the ground. As the little bird fluttered helplessly and the ten-year-old wailed, the gray predator ripped open the top of the finch's head and ate its brains. Then it shot up to the top of a tree.

There the Wibergs got their first good look at the cruel gray beast.

It was no monster. It was a songbird.

Though shaped and colored much like a mocking bird, it had a distinctive broad black stripe through the eye—masked like a bandit—and a sharp beak, curved like an eagle's. From these field markings, Wiberg realized they'd witnessed an attack by the infamous Butcher Bird of the North: a.k.a., the northern shrike.

Solitary and wary, this tiny predator is relatively rare and visits us only in winter—which is fortunate for the small creatures who frequent lawns, orchards, and grasslands. Perched high in a tree, sitting upright like a hawk, the northern shrike considers most little birds and mammals fair game: chickadees, titmice, finches, sparrows, voles, mice—it will even kill prey larger than itself, including big blue jays, starlings, and rats.

A predatory songbird is a disturbing enough concept. (Although as Massachusetts Audubon ornithologist Simon Perkins points out, other songbirds are carnivorous—including worm-eating robins.) But what the shrike does after killing its prey is even more unsettling: often, it will fly to a perch beside a thorn or along some barbed wire, and then carefully skewer the victim there, leaving it impaled like some furred or feathered cocktail frank.

As Martha Stewart might remind us, the most memorable aspect of a meal is often the presentation. The sight of some chickadee or vole thus impaled does seem to linger in the mind like a scene from a Stephen King movie.

"If you didn't know better, you'd think it had been done by some brutal little kids," says Kenn Kaufman, author of *Lives of North American Birds*. "You'd think, oh, it's awful," he says—and then he pauses, to consider for a moment: "And it sort of is."

Certainly small birds and mammals would concur. On a February morning a few years ago, Dave Winter looked out at his Dedham back yard and found, to his astonishment, a tableaux of animals frozen in fear: a downy woodpecker hugged the trunk of a thorn tree, bill in mid-peck against the bark; a gray squirrel backed up against a branch; two chickadees and a titmouse clung motionless to twigs; and a goldfinch perched, unmoving, in an oak. "They all remained motionless for a measured twenty-five minutes," the naturalist noted in his field journal. What could inspire such terror? That winter, as periodically happens for reasons unknown, an unusual number of shrikes flew south from Canada to New England. At least one of them had been haunting his bird feeder for two months.

Terrorizing back yard bird feeders, impaling mice, making

little girls cry—no wonder the shrike is, even among bird lovers, sometimes *avis non grata*. In the 1870s, the Boston Common hired a shrike warden to protect its newly introduced house sparrows from the depredations of this avian Vlad the Impaler. (In the winter of 1878–79, Kaufman reports, the warden succeeded in shooting no fewer than fifty of them.)

"Man is very prejudiced against the shrikes—always have been," laments Reuben Yosef. As Global Coordinator of the International Shrike Working Group, a group of four hundred "shrikers" studying the dozens of different kinds of shrikes world-wide, the Israel-based Yosef would like to counteract the bad PR. "They are beautiful birds," he insists, "with a role to play in nature, and their behavior is unique in the animal world."

To a biologist, the shrikes' unique enthusiasm for impaling other creatures is as intriguing as it is gruesome. The behavior almost certainly first evolved to help these little birds eat. Though they act like birds of prey, butcher birds lack the tearing talons of hawks, owls, and eagles. They use those skewers to help them eat their meal the way we use knife and fork.

But that's not the whole story, as Yosef discovered studying shrikes in Israel (the same species, incidentally, as our New England shrike.) Male butcher birds seem to have evolved a second use for impaling prey: not only do the skewers serve as cutlery, but also as grizzly advertisements of their hunting prowess to potential mates.

Males impale more prey than do females, and they do so especially during the breeding season. At that time, the birds may skewer not only the usual rats, snakes, scorpions, and lizards, but also pieces of cloth and eggshells. Yosef suspected the most conspicuous displays would attract the most females.

Yosef set out to test his idea. Like a crazed Robin Hood, the researcher robbed impaled prey from "rich" male shrikes, and then skewered the stolen items on thorns in the territories of less fortunate shrikes. The result? Female shrikes, like wise women all over the world, followed the larder. Not only did the males with more prey attract more mates than did the victims of

Yosef's depredations—their mates also laid more eggs!

Male shrikes' efforts to impress females lead Yosef to another discovery, this time with American shrikes. Among the prey items posted on the thorn trees he surveyed in Florida were conspicuous black, red, and yellow grasshoppers. Yosef took them to an entomologist to be identified. "It's impossible!" he was told. "There is no way a bird killed this to eat it." The insects were Lubber's grasshoppers—insects who can afford to be large, ponderous, and gregarious because they excrete a pungent poison. Because no creature was known to eat these grasshoppers, entomologists christened their poison "nature's most perfect defense."

Until shrikes figured out a way around it. The poison, as it turns out, breaks down after death, when the grasshopper carcass turns brown. And indeed, that's when shrikes eat them. Yosef suspects that shrikes initially hunted the insects for display only—"window dressing, just to catch the eye"—and later discovered that their display could be eaten.

In his 1925 classic, *A Natural History of American Birds*, New England ornithologist Edward Howe Forbush admonishes us to respect the northern shrike. "Though we may deplore his attack on smaller birds," he writes, "we can but admire his self-reliance, audacity, and courage." To that already impressive list we can now add the shrike's astonishing adaptability—perhaps the most crucial asset for this tiny, singing predator.

Otters

Infectious Joy, Ecstatic Grace

*O*n a beautiful winter day, after one of the first good snows
of the season, Don and Lillian Stokes set out to look for animal tracks to draw and include in their book, *A Guide to Animal
Tracking and Behavior*.

They hadn't even left the parking lot of the Great Meadows
Wildlife Refuge in the city of Concord, Massachusetts when they
encountered a mystery: a trough, about eight inches wide, ran
across the lot and then directly into some dense brush. A child's
toboggan? But why sled into the underbrush? Intrigued, they
followed the trough. Where it ended, tracks began—paw prints
as big as a dog's, but with webbed feet.

The naturalists were astonished. Here, in a parking lot only
twenty miles from Boston, they come upon the path of a 6-foot-
long, 25-pound animal who'd been sledding on its belly through
the snow. The paw prints left no question: this was a wild river
otter, one of the most playful, athletic, and appealing mammals
anywhere on earth.

"We had previously thought we had to be in real wilderness
before we ever saw otter tracks," Don Stokes confessed. That's a
common assumption. "Most people don't even realize there are
otters in many, many towns you don't commonly associate with
wildlife," says Erik Amati, a game biologist with Massachusetts
Fish and Wildlife.

But, in fact, "around just about any stream in Massachusetts, you can find otter signs," says Tom Decker, a wildlife biologist with the Massachusetts Division of Fish and Wildlife.

Thanks to the Clean Water Act, controls on fur trapping, and the hard work of beavers—yes, beavers—otter populations have been steadily climbing for the past thirty years, Decker explains. What's the beavers' contribution? Their skillfully engineered waterways create ideal conditions for aquatic otters. (Female otters even give birth inside abandoned beaver lodges.) After a long respite from trapping, the Northeast's once-beleaguered beavers have staged a comeback—and so, too, have the otters.

"Go out to an old beaver flowage or a slowly flowing stream or an old or a new beaver dam, and just sit and watch," advises Amati: you might well spot a sleek, dark-brown, torpedo-shaped water weasel cavort across the dam. Winter's snow records their movements, and makes their dark forms easier to see.

You might see one pop out of a hole in the ice like a jack-in-the-box, or hauled out on the snow, chewing a fish, eating the head first. (You can hear the bones crunching seventy-five feet away. Though otters eat mostly fish, their strong jaws can also crack the shells of big turtles and easily crush crustaceans.)

The greatest reward of a sighting is the chance to watch these joyful, graceful creatures at play. Twirling, rolling, chasing, sliding, otters play with equal zest alone or with others, in water, on ice, and in snow. Otters are so fun-loving they are known to keep toys in their dens: stones or shells or sticks that they like to drop through the water and chase. They often choose the rapids of a river to slip under the ice and ride the racing water.

Otter slides vividly report some rollicking good toboggan runs: Sue Morse, founder and director of the nonprofit wildlife monitoring organization, Keeping Track, once measured a slide near her home in Jericho, Vermont that stretched for twenty-six feet. "It wasn't just a belly flop with a trough of snow," she explained. From the occasional track alongside the slide, "I could see the otter was trying to get the most out of the ride, and propelled itself along with its feet, just like a person riding on a sled," she said. "I actually laughed out loud, even though I was alone!"

Otters' apparent joy is infectious. Former trapper John Kulish, who observed otters for more than sixty years, recalled watching an otter pop up repeatedly through the slush ice of a New Hampshire pond, each time with a fish in its mouth. Each time it would explode through the slush like a black torpedo, bob its head, spin the fish around, toss it in the air, crunch it up, then pop back down again—to reappear minutes later, fifty feet away, with a new fish. "I can't decide whether it most enjoyed the fishing, the spinning, the eating, or the popping!" Kulish said.

But these sleek athletes are more than just playful clowns. Otters, like minks, skunks, and wolverines, are members of the weasel family, a clan known for their strength, courage, and tenacity. With powerful jaws and sharp teeth, an otter can kill a dog of similar size. It can run as fast as eighteen miles an hour. Traveling rivers, even when it must break through thin ice to breathe, an otter can swim more than fifteen miles a day.

Although otters often travel alone, they are social creatures, sometimes gathering in groups of up to eight animals to play and fish. To keep up with neighbors' whereabouts, and to advertise their own, otters often leave their fishy-smelling scats, glittering with fish scales, on prominent rocks, logs, or mounds. These latrines seem to function as bulletin boards on which every visitor leaves a calling card identified with a powerful, distinctive scent from glands beneath the tail. (Dogs apparently find the scent irresistible and will roll in these piles in seeming ecstasy.) When these latrines are placed along the borders of two otters' territories, you may find as many as thirty or forty along a half-mile stretch.

Otters, like people, keep track of members of their own family for life (which may last fourteen years or more.) Kits stay with their mothers, usually with the father close by, for their first year and a half before striking out on their own. Otter parents are devoted lovers who mate for life, and, Kulish was convinced, mourn the death of a loved one. Several times over his trapping career, Kulish found surviving otters repeatedly returning to the site where he had trapped a mate or offspring. Invariably he would find the survivor, even weeks later, neither fishing nor playing, but apparently searching for the lost ones.

He especially remembered a family of three he had targeted along New Hampshire's Contoocook River. He caught the adult male and the yearling son. But where was the mother? Two weeks later, he found her: she was swimming and diving, but without flourish. She gazed unwaveringly toward the site of his traps. Each time she surfaced, she let out a series of four or five plaintive, dove-like sounds.

It was she, he said, that convinced him to trap otters no more.

"As a man, I would like to be the kind of man an otter is as an animal," he said many years later. "I first learned to enjoy their play; then to respect their intelligence; next to admire their character—and finally, to love them for the rare and noble creatures that they are."

The Not-So-Private
Life of Pigeons

ॐ

*E*ven on the coldest days of January, when the rest of nature seems to have deserted the city, they offer a spectacle of wildness and wonder right at your feet.

Strutting, feeding, bobbing, bossing, flirting, fleeing, fighting, lovemaking—you name it—these birds' complex lives unfold before us in intimate detail. You don't have to wait until spring to see intricate courtship behaviors or even nesting—they do it practically year-round. And you can watch them with ease, without binoculars, from a park bench or a window.

These creatures sound like the answer to every bird watcher's prayer. Until, that is, you pronounce their name: pigeons.

"I know, I know," says Mariane Schonfisch, "everybody says the same thing about pigeons: they're dirty, diseased, rats with wings." Schonfisch, who researched people's views of pigeons for a Sociology of the Environment class at San Jose State University, recently watched a grandmother teaching her grandson to feed the ducks at a park—and to kick at the pigeons.

"They're universally despised," she said, "up there with cockroaches and rats."

Our contempt far exceeds our familiarity with these intelligent creatures, which outperform many mammals on complex tests in psychologists' laboratories. The lives of city pigeons are as mysterious as the birds are ubiquitous—simply because we consider them beneath our notice.

Yet a creature of nobler heritage can hardly be imagined. Here, at our feet on the Boston Common, taking bread from our hands at virtually every park in every city of the world, is the very bird that brought Caesar news of his victories, the same species that taught Darwin the fundamentals of genetics. The dove that brought Noah the olive branch and has served as a symbol of peace through the centuries may well have been a pigeon—for city pigeons are actually a species of dove, known as a rock dove, which originated in the Middle East.

"It might not be too much to say that man's imagination first navigated the air on the wings of a Middle Eastern rock dove," Steven J. Bodio, who grew up racing pigeons with the Dorchester Homing Pigeon Club, writes in his book, *Aloft*.

Easily trained, pigeons were the first birds humans domesticated, even before chickens; yet they were always able to fly free, acting as their owners' sky probes. As early as 4500 BC, people raised rock doves for meat, and later for carrying messages, especially for armies. So efficient were these strong, swift fliers that news of Napoleon's defeat at Waterloo reached England by pigeon four days in advance of news carried by horse and ship.

But what do pigeons do when they're not busy running errands for us? About this we know startlingly little—but we may be about to find out. Project PigeonWatch is the nationwide volunteer research program of Cornell's Laboratory of Ornithology, the Ithaca-based international center for the study and conservation of birds.

Why would such a respected institution be messing around with pigeons? Shouldn't they be studying some weird auk or exotic woodpecker instead? "We forget to look at pigeons as city wildlife," says Martha Fisher, Project PigeonWatch coordinator.

"But they're an accessible species which can help us answer very real scientific questions, and could help us understand other birds as well."

Among the questions the study seeks to answer is what role color variation plays in the lives of birds in different habitats.

Why can you count up to seven different colors of pigeons in city flocks—from mainly white to mostly red to browns, pinks and blues—while flocks of the same species, living in the country, are invariably all bluish with the same grayish wing bar (a form known as a "blue bar")?

Perhaps different colors flourish in cities because cities shelter fewer predators like hawks and owls (though Boston and New York do have peregrine falcons). In the city, perhaps a pigeon can better afford to stand out and not be eaten. Or perhaps certain colors rank "higher" than others in a flock. Perhaps only those flocks enjoying the most abundant resources (cities offer plenty of food) can afford to contain a mix of colors.

These are the sorts of questions that can be explored by counting the numbers of pigeons of each color in different flocks, observing the birds' behavior, and recording it. Which color pigeons get first dibs on bread crumbs spread before the flock? Do pigeons choose others of the same color as mates? (It's easy to spot a pigeon courting: with neck feathers ruffled, the male lowers his head and turns in circles, spreads and drags his tail with head high, and chases the female. While the female may also bow and circle, she doesn't chase the male.)

What we know about wild pigeons so far suggests that PigeonWatch volunteers are in for a spectacle of romance and intrigue. "Pigeons are monogamous, but there's also a lot of fooling around," Fisher observes.

A single city block may constitute a pigeon Peyton Place: some preliminary research in Syracuse, New York suggests that while a pigeon's eye may wander, the flock doesn't. The Syracuse flock in question never strayed even two blocks away.

The reason pigeons can afford to court and mate and raise young during all four seasons is these birds don't depend on spring's abundance to feed their young. Pigeons, and also flamingos, are able to feed their nestlings from secretions of their own bodies. "Pigeon milk"—a cottage-cheese-like secretion of the bird's crop (the organ at the top of the digestive system)—is chemically similar to mammalian breast milk. Both parents produce this "milk," and it's the only food the nestlings need for the first days of life. Later it supplements other items the parents regurgitate to the nestlings in the stiff stick nests along building ornaments, ledges, and bridges.

Milk-making without mammaries is but one of pigeons' impressive feats. In psychologists' laboratories, they have shown conceptual abilities—recognizing, for instance, as "human" projected slides of people of all races, ages, and sizes as well as just a face, hand, or foot. They have even mastered every letter of the Roman alphabet.

Yet these are mere parlor tricks compared to the birds' ability to "home," which is born of a complex of extraordinary extensions of the senses and which scientists are only beginning to explore. Laboratory experiments show that pigeons can see infrared light, hear ultra-low-frequency sounds, sense the earth's magnetic field, smell subtle currents of airborne scent, and interpret all this information to help them find destinations hundreds, sometimes thousands of miles from a release site.

Canned Wildlife

Weird Lessons from the Tube and Silver Screen

࿐

*O*utside, in nature, cold rain splashes on dirty ice. But inside, on *Nature*, zebras gallop and graze on a televised savanna only inches from a comfortable armchair.

On wet wintry days, no wonder some of us would rather learn about wildlife from a screen. Problem is, we may have learned the wrong lessons, and learned them too well.

Though many folks can't identify the winter song of a chickadee, almost everyone knows the call of the jungle. The same, distinctive cry has opened nearly every tropical wildlife show since *Ramar of the Jungle*, the 1952 TV series starring John Hall as the scientist adventuring through Africa and India. It goes, "Ooo,ooo,ooo,ooo! Ah,ah,Ah,AH-AH!"

Most people assume it's the call of some monkey. Actually, it's the voice of a critter that never set foot in a jungle: the kookaburra, an Australian kingfisher that perches in gum trees and laughs out the familiar syllables as it flies.

Maybe now we can guess what it's laughing about: how Hollywood and even some documentary filmmakers have us woefully confused over how real wildlife acts, looks, and sounds.

"It can really send a big message that's totally wrong about the natural world," says Sue Knapp, senior publicist at the New England Aquarium. She's still smarting from the natural history

197

debacle of Paramount's 1994 film *Andre*, a movie inspired by
New England's favorite harbor seal.

Until he died at age twenty-five in 1986, Andre the seal
delighted New Englanders from Connecticut to Maine. He
wintered at either the New England Aquarium or the Mystic
Marinelife Aquarium in Connecticut; but each spring, he swam
north to spend the warm months in Maine with the Rockport
family who had adopted him as an orphan, amusing townsfolk
and tourists with his aquatic tricks.

Paramount touted the film as "based on a true story." But the
story wasn't Andre's: in the movie, the famous seal is played by
an utterly different species—a California sea lion.

The real Andre was five feet long and weighed 250 pounds.
Sea lions are more than twice that size. Harbor seals' coats are
spotted gray; sea lions' are a uniform, chocolate brown. Harbor
seals' ears look like little holes. Sea lions have ear flaps. Harbor
seals spend almost their whole lives in the water. Sea lions spend
lots of time on land, galloping over rocks using their huge front
flippers. Casting a sea lion as Andre, said Aquarium marine
mammalogist Greg Early, was "like a remake of Moby Dick
using a sheep for the whale. It just made no sense."

But it made sense to Hollywood. "There are no seals in the
biz who can do anything for you," explains Robert Bloch, owner
and operator of Los Angeles-based Critters of the Cinema, one of
thirty-three suppliers of trained animals for TV in California
(which is, not surprisingly, the center for the industry). Though
seals are just as smart as sea lions, "Seals can't get around on the
ground. They flop around on their bellies." And since the film
crew and the human actors were all terrestrial, a real seal's real
water tricks just wouldn't cut it. That's why the star of *The
Golden Seal*, which came out the previous year, was also played
by a sea lion. Even the trained "seals" you used to see in circuses
were really sea lions.

Similar logistics explain why a South American capuchin
monkey manages to bring a deadly African virus to America in
Outbreak. Capuchins are readily available and easily trained;
most African primates of similar size are difficult to obtain and
less tractable, explains Bloch.

Such practical matters also dictated that a trained chimp play one of the gorillas in Universal/Warner Brothers' 1988 *Gorillas in the Mist*. Though the movie was shot on location in Rwanda among wild mountain gorillas, in one sequence Sigourney Weaver, playing primatologist Dian Fossey, holds a baby gorilla in her arms. Wild mountain gorilla mothers won't stand for that, and there are no trained gorillas "in the biz" (no koalas, either). The solution? Central casting found a young chimp with acting credits and dressed him up in a gorilla suit.

Availability and trainability—not authenticity—explain many casting choices for Hollywood pictures. Alligators, domestic and docile, usually play crocodiles. Iguanas play most lizards. Tigers, native to Asia, often play the Big Cat role in films set in Africa instead of lions, because adult male lions are so difficult to train that "there are only two reliable lions at the moment in the biz," says Bloch (though there are plenty of good lionesses and even more good tigers, he adds).

Feature films can claim artistic license. Documentary films are supposed to be another matter. But even they can't always be trusted.

Watching a recent television documentary about sea turtles, Massachusetts Audubon ornithologist Wayne Petersen saw frigate birds swoop down to gobble up just-hatched baby turtles on their way to the sea. True enough; but each time a frigate swooped, the soundtrack played a ringing, wild call. Petersen immediately recognized the banshee-wail of the limpkin—a wading bird that eats only freshwater snails.

But where was the call of the frigate bird? "The problem is," said Petersen, "the frigate bird doesn't say much of anything."

Perhaps the sound track was an honest mix-up. Failing to match accurate sound with picture "is the easiest single kind of mistake you can make," says John Rubin, a supervising producer at National Geographic Television's Natural History Unit, which is renowned for its dedication to accuracy.

Most people don't realize that movie cameras don't have built-in mikes like videocams do. Sound is recorded with a separate machine, heavy and complicated enough that it ordinarily requires the full attention of a sound recordist. But to minimize disturbance to sensitive wildlife, explains Rubin, many natural history documentaries are shot silently by a lone cameraman instead of a whole film crew, and he tries to record sound between film takes. Unfortunately few wild animals are considerate enough to offer their entire vocal repertoires to the mike at that time. Further, while a 600mm zoom lens can pick up a faraway image, no microphone can record the sounds the animal makes at that distance, unless it is a very loud sound.

So production houses use sound libraries—collections of tapes and CDs—to provide real-life noises to be added as needed. Some collections, such as the BBC's and the Library of Natural Sounds at Cornell's Laboratory of Ornithology, are detailed and extensive. Others are rather generic: most productions use the same tape for all engine ignitions—a Chrysler car—and for helicopter—a Bell "Huey." Many use the same generic tape of "desert sounds," which, incongruously, features the call of a loon—because that's what Hollywood thinks the desert ought to sound like. "Frog songs" feature the California tree frog, which is why we think—mistakenly—that all frogs say "Ribbit." Actually, only this one species does.

To add animal sounds to his documentary *Yellowstone: Realm of the Coyote,* Rubin consulted a sound library. He recalls his delight the first time he watched the film with the sound dubbed in. "The star coyote opens his mouth, and out comes a beautiful howl. It was so delightful after all that time to finally hear my character speak." Rubin's collaborator, a coyote expert, agreed: "That's really lovely," he told Rubin in the editing room, "—but it's a wolf howl."

Rubin corrected the error well before the film was aired. He discovered the tape he'd been sent had been mis-labelled.

"When viewers watch our movies, they expect us to be completely accurate," explains Scott Wyerman, Director of Research at National Geographic television. "The truth that we're documenting is more fascinating than anything Hollywood could make up."

Only one thing beats a first-rate wildlife documentary: getting outside and seeing the real, wild world for yourself.

Where Do Bugs Go in Winter?

*O*ne winter day in southern New Hampshire, a visitor asked an ice fisherman how he could possibly enjoy sitting by a hole in the middle of a frozen lake.

The fisherman's answer was simple: "Mosquitoes aren't a bother."

For the entomologically inhibited, winter's winning feature is its lack of bugs. But where have they gone?

"What about caterpillars?" asks the poet, Aileen Fisher,

> "Where do they crawl
> When the stars say Frost
> and the trees say Fall?"

A few caterpillars, like those who turn into monarchs, solve the problem of winter by flying to Mexico. Some dragonflies, like the familiar green darner and the peripatetic wandering globetrotter, migrate, sometimes by the millions, to winter in Florida.

But most insects actually stick around. In the fall, many insects, like us, seek out and seal up their shelters for winter. The reason you don't notice them is they would rather not be found, and some go to elaborate lengths to stay hidden.

"Winter is a dangerous time for insects," says Robert Childs, an entomologist at the University of Massachusetts, Amherst. It's a wonder they can survive at all: most insects are less than an inch long, fragile enough to be squashed with a finger, and cold-blooded to boot. But, as Childs observes, "insects have been around 400 million years. They've seen just about everything the earth has to offer, and they're incredibly adaptable."

Insects have perfected the art of surviving cold weather, with an astonishing array of strategies. Some survive by turning into something else: the larva of the showy cecropia moth transforms itself into a chrysalis, a fist-sized gray silken pouch you might find hanging at the tip of a birch or alder at the edge of a swamp.

Many insects even go so far as to change the contents of their blood for the season: they replace much of their normal body fluids with glycerol, similar to the glycol used in automobile antifreeze. Some also thicken their blood. These measures, reports Melody Kenna, a Forest Service research entomologist at Hamden, Connecticut, can lower the freezing point of their body fluids to -47° Centigrade.

Thanks to this chemistry, the familiar black and brown woolly bear caterpillar (the larvae of a tiger moth) can wait out the snow under just a few inches of leaf litter; sawflies hide just beneath logs; and the fragile violet-brown mourning cloak butterfly survives almost completely exposed. With wings closed, showing only its drab undersides, it is nearly invisible against logs or the dark bark of trees. And after a punishing winter, it is one of the first insects to fly again in spring, often before the snow melts. (You can tell individuals who have made it through the winter by the white margin on the wings; newly hatched butterflies sport broad yellow wing margins.)

Other insects construct ingenious shelters, like the larch case bearer. If you look carefully, you'll see them on larch trees, also known as tamaracks, the needle-bearing trees that turn gold and then, unlike most conifers, shed their needles in the fall. The insects look exactly like the tips of dead needles. That's because when they hatch in July, these ⅛-inch-long creatures hollow out the tip of a needle, back into it, and wear it around like a camouflaged suit of armor. When the needles fall off the tree, they move to the branches and cluster there for the winter, invisible to predators. Many species of leaf-rollers employ a similar strategy.

You'll know one of these caterpillars was at work when you notice among your leaf pile a leaf that looks like a hand-rolled cigar.

Like the "summer people" who vacate their lakeside cottages, other insects vacate their warm-weather shelters for their winter homes. Those holes you find in acorns on the ground were made by acorn weevils. At the Entomological Society of America, the acorn weevil is one of public relations coordinator Brian Fitzek's favorite animals, because they can make such a good science project for kids.

If you collect a bunch of acorns and put them in water, those that float are most likely to contain weevil larvae, he advises. If you carefully open one, you'll find two to four worm-like baby weevils inside. Earlier in the summer, the female weevil drilled a hole through the developing acorn's shell to lay her eggs inside. When they hatch, the babies feed on the nutmeat. But when the acorn drops, it's a rude awakening for the little beasts. They take it as a signal to begin chewing their way out—a process that Donald Stokes reports in his *Guide to Observing Insect Lives* may occupy them for up to three days.

Fitzek advises you can watch this process if you keep your unopened floating acorns in a jar on a damp towel. (Normally the weevil larva would then dig into the soil and spend up to five winters there before emerging as an adult—a quarter-inch, light brown, long-snouted character who looks like Gonzo on *Sesame Street*.)

Many of the most conspicuous insect nests you're likely to spot in the fall are empty. The big sticky nests of tent caterpillars, who build the structures at the forks of tree branches, and those of the fall web worms, whose nests are found at the tips, have both been vacated. If you open one up, you'll find only shed caterpillars skins and their droppings. The caterpillars spend the winter as pupae, encased in a light cocoon situated under loose bark or fallen leaves. If you find a dead caterpillar in the nest, it's likely the victim of an ichneumon wasp, which lays its eggs on the caterpillar. The hatching wasps feed on the caterpillar and kill it.

Other insects vacate their summer homes only to move into yours. Hundreds of Asian multicolored lady beetles fly to the south-facing walls of white houses on warm fall days, making their way up to the attic. Cluster flies slip through tiny cracks to winter in barns, garages, and attics, too, causing dismay in the spring when they buzz at the windows, trying to get back out. Box elder bugs, $\frac{3}{8}$-inch-long insects with orange marks on the perimeter of the wings, also swarm to the sides of houses, trying to get in. (Even though these bugs are harmless, some homeowners find them so annoying they cut down the nearest female box elder to get rid of them, eliminating the seeds upon which the bugs feed.)

Of course, another way to deal with winter is to just die— which actually works fine for some species as long as they make a point of laying eggs first. The little brown balls you find in cobwebs are the egg sacs of spiders; an inch-long, purse like structure on a twig or stem that looks like brown styrofoam is the egg sac of the praying mantis. Hundreds of babies will burst out when the weather warms back up—just in time to catch other insects as they dig up, hatch out, or migrate back in the spring.

Ice Storm

The Silver Lining of Disaster

A few years back, our January ice storms made history. "Unprecedented" was how the federal Forest Service described it in a brief for the governors of the four hardest-hit states. In Maine, Vermont, New Hampshire, and New York, thirty-seven counties were declared federal disaster areas. About one-fifth of the vast northern forest is believed to have lost most or all its trees. The Federal Emergency Management Agency compares the ice storm damage to that of the Hurricane of 1938.

Though the power's long been restored and downed trees cleared from city streets, the Ice Storm of 1998 continues to change the course of history—the unwritten natural history of creatures from mice to moose, from orchids to owls.

"There are a lot of ramifications to events that are this wide-spread," says Dave Houston, a researcher recently retired from the U.S. Forest Service's Center for Forest Health Research in Hamden, Connecticut. "A storm like this has implications and affects relationships that you don't think about—on and on!"

The storm's legacy ushered in spectacular blooms of pink lady slippers the following spring. It caused some squirrels to starve the next fall. But it also meant that grouse would enjoy better habitat for years to come, and that perhaps up to a decade later, woodpeckers will flock to New England in numbers never before counted.

In fact, an ice storm can subtly but profoundly shape the landscape well into the middle of the next century.

But then again, it may not.

"There's a lot we don't know," says Houston. But for researchers, therein lies the opportunity. "The storm was so widespread and so destructive, it crossed many forest types, from high mountains to low swamps, and it will afford a chance to document many habitats' responses. This storm provided a lot of people a big laboratory so they can go out and answer a lot of questions we've wondered about," he says.

And for some wildlife species, the storm, violent as it was, created opportunities, too. "There are definitely some positive aspects," stresses Jim Speilman, a forester at the Forest Service's Natural Resources Conservation Service in Durham, New Hampshire. "The way people react to it isn't the same way nature reacts to it."

For some animals, though, an ice storm of this magnitude was a disaster—at least in the short term. Grouse were surely among the worst casualties. These game birds often roost in snow, snuggling into drifts like a person in a down comforter. But the grouse that snow-roosted on those punishing January nights were entombed by the ice. "They turned into grousesicles," said Mariko Yamasaki, research wildlife biologist at the U.S. Forest Service's Forest Science Lab in Durham.

Wild turkeys, on the other hand, fared far better. Deep snow, not ice, is a turkey's weather nightmare. The hardy bird can survive two weeks without eating—and there's usually something to eat anyway. They'll pick grain out of manure or visit back yard bird feeders if need be, and a flock can easily travel ten miles in a day—if they don't have to walk through snow.

But for critters who cache their food in the ground, ice cuts off their larder. Squirrels and blue jays can't dig up their food—and with those who starve dies the memories of where they buried their nuts and seeds. And that means huge numbers of oak and beech seedlings the following spring.

For other animals, an ice storm brings manna from heaven: a cascade of woody debris. "We don't like it because it makes walking through it work," says Yamasaki, "but for wildlife, this sort of thing is great." Downed branches and twigs offer fine cover for mice, shrews, and some birds—and these species in turn draw their predators, like weasels, fishers, and martens. Deer and moose feast on fallen buds and bark. (Though for the deer and moose, that benefit is outweighed when persistent ice impedes their escape from coyotes and dogs. And the broken buds may also mean bad news for seed-eating species. More bad news for gray squirrels and jays, not to mention deer, white footed mice, and red-headed woodpeckers is that those missing flower buds can't set seed the next fall.) Come spring and summer, the debris will offer moist, shady shelter for terrestrial salamanders, newts, and snakes.

Damage to the crowns of so many trees can considerably alter conditions on the ground. With the canopy cracked, once-shady forest floors may flood with sunlight. The extra sunlight will coax spectacular spring blooms of pink lady slippers and trailing arbutus from the forest.

In forests with the heaviest damage, "thousands and thousands of acres of new habitat will be created," says Dick DeGraaf, a research biologist with the Massachusetts Division of Fisheries and Wildlife. Five to ten years after the storm, areas denuded of trees should be colonized by blackberries and raspberries—rich resources for shrub-nesting birds like veeries and catbirds and grouse. New species of saplings may next appear among the shrubbery. Light-tolerant ash, suggests Houston, may show up where ice downed big maples and pines. Large openings in the canopy and soil disturbances from falling debris may encourage birch and aspen seeds to sprout.

New habitats may also be opening up in the damaged trees still standing. And unless people unwisely cut down too many damaged trees, the ice storm of '98 will, eventually, dramatically increase some of the most sought-after niches in nature: tree hollows.

Sheltering a suite of animals from nesting woodpeckers to wood ducks, from hibernating bears to day-roosting bats, these valuable hideaways form only after trees are wounded.

Depending on the attentions of creatures such as beetles and woodpeckers, good-size holes and hollows may appear in beeches and aspens within a year or two of damage. Snapped-off pine branches may turn into hollows within a couple of years. Oaks may take decades to create good-size hollows favored by big animals such as porcupines and bears. Yamasaki says we may well be surprised, five to ten years after a big ice storm, to discover a welcome flush of colorful woodpeckers.

But what may surprise us most may be how quickly nature recovers from even the most punishing weather. Forester Speilman notes that a healthy tree can lose a quarter of its crown without setback. Some trees can survive the loss of nearly three-quarters of the crown. Many trees actually benefit from some pruning, as orchardists well know. (One Forest Service study suggests that when many oaks are felled, surviving oaks may bear more acorns in poor mast years—when wildlife need them most.)

And remember: even dead trees give life to wild animals. "Don't cut every tree that's damaged," Yamasaki urges. "It's all part of the mix we need to maintain wildlife."

Don't view an ice storm as a disaster, she advises. It's all part of nature's dynamism. "There's obvious personal property damage, and I'm not trivializing that," she says. "But disturbance—wind, fire, ice—stirs the pot. For wildlife, opportunities develop. We just have to wait to see what they are."

Fishers Stage a Comeback

ॐ

*I*n the winter, some of the commonest tracks you may find in the woods belong to a creature most people never see, many never suspect, and some mistake for a bloodthirsty monster.

A crazy quilt of footprints in the snow tells of a frenetically inquisitive creature, bounding, circling, walking, loping, pouncing, rocketing up trees and down—sometimes all within thirty feet. The $2\frac{1}{2}$-inch-long tracks are about the size of a fox's, but five toes show instead of four. The changing gaits and directions reflect the adventures of a fisher—a tree-dwelling weasel whose fur outshines the mink's and whose grace outranks the otter's.

The fisher's lustrous brown fur helped trappers pay off the Plymouth Plantation settlers' debts to Europe. Even three centuries later, in the 1980s, a fisher coat might fetch $10,000 in Paris. But when the coat is left on the fisher, the luxuriant fur clothes "a sculptured sleekness that reveals an inward, controlled power and strength," as the late Cameron Langford wrote in his book, *The Winter of the Fisher*. The fisher's grace reminded the author of "willows weeping in the wind."

Above all, its hunting prowess earns the fisher a reputation as a predator par excellence. Astonishingly strong for such a small animal (females weigh only six pounds; a big male perhaps twice that), the fisher is so skilled that, with a few well-placed nips to the face and neck, it can kill a porcupine quicker than the rodent can slap its quills.

You might think such a storied creature would only be found in deep wilderness. But in New England, "there are fishers in Worcester, fishers in Concord, fishers ten miles outside of Boston," says Tom Decker, a biologist with the Massachusetts Division of Fisheries and Wildlife.

By the turn of the century, over-trapping and treecutting had wiped out most of New England's fishers. Now, though, with forests regrowing and trapping restricted, this swift, graceful weasel of the north woods has made a spectacular comeback. Sizeable fisher populations can be found throughout Northern New England, as well as in the Adirondacks, Michigan, Wisconsin, Minnesota, and the forests of Canada. Massachusetts boasts some of the highest densities of fishers in North America. Some areas might have a fisher every two square miles. New Hampshire and Maine have so many they've helped re-stock five other states.

Still, most folks have never heard of fishers. Those who have, may have heard the wrong thing: that they're huge, vicious cats that assault livestock, house cats, and schoolbuses, then shriek all night.

In fact, fishers are only three feet long (including the tail), surprisingly gentle with people, and unrelated to cats (except as fellow carnivores; they're in the weasel family with otters). As for the shriek you heard at night, though fishers can utter bloodcurdling screams, so can almost everybody else—including rabbits, deer, and (the most likely source of nighttime yowls) house cats.

Yet the legends persist. Old-timers (the ones you ask "have you lived here all your life" and they reply "not yet") warn you about the so-called "fisher cat" that can "take down a hoss!" Even one mammalogy textbook reports that a fisher can kill a grown deer. At New Hampshire Fish and Game, fur bearer biologist Eric Orff fields queries from panicked citizens: "I have kids, I have livestock, and a fisher has been reported in the area. What should I do?"

"Yes, fishers are vicious," Orff tells them, "—if you're a mouse, a squirrel, or a raccoon. If you're much bigger than that, you can relax."

A study completed last year found that, in central Massachusetts at least, red and gray squirrels are at the top of the fisher's menu. (In fact, some fishers take over squirrel nests and use them as day beds after eating the occupants.) The thin, pointed scats, often found beneath the tall tree hollows where fishers like to den, catalogue an eclectic diet: you can find the skins and seeds of fruits and nuts, the carapaces of beetles, the feathers of wild turkeys, the hair and bones of raccoons—and yes, though rarely, perhaps the remains of a house cat. ("In their diet," assures Decker, "house cats are like a trace element.") You might find deer hair, too, which is surely what threw off the authors of that mammalogy text. No fisher ever killed an adult deer, though it will gladly scavenge a carcass.

And fishers don't fish. The name is probably a corruption of the word fitch, the name for the pelt of the fisher's continental relative, the European polecat.

Follow some fisher tracks and you might find what it ate that day. One snowy morning, Meade Cadot, who directs the Harris Center for Conservation Education in Hancock, New Hampshire, did just that. He followed the winding tracks on snowshoes until he found a pounce mark and a hole in the snow. "There, I found the fisher's victim," Cadot said. "It had killed an apple."

As the principal investigator of the Massachusetts fisher study, University of Massachusetts Amhurst student Eric York did Cadot one better: from 1992–1995, he radio collared ninety-three fishers, and followed them around.

He found some, particularly the young, journeyed so far that he needed a plane to track the signal. Some, investigating every inch of the way, set up new territories sixty miles from where they were first captured in northern Worcester County. Several crossed the Connecticut River into Vermont and New Hampshire (via bridges; despite their name, fishers don't like water).

Then in May of 1995, one of his collared fishers was hit by a car. It was a female whose den York had planned to check the next day. Inside he found three hungry kits. So, like wildlife cinematographer Marty Stouffer did a few years back, York took the kits home to raise and to study.

The male of the litter died, but the two female kits thrived in a pen York built behind his parents' farmhouse in Shelburne. First they drank milk from a bottle, then they ate chopped liver and cat food. When York began to offer live prey—a neighbor's unwanted rooster—he was deeply impressed with the young fishers' technique. He'd grown up on a farm, where butchered chickens running about headless were a common, though dis-comforting, sight. The fishers had a better idea: one quick bite to the back of the head, "and that chicken would lay right down." (Unlike the farmer who severs the spinal cord after the neurolog-ical message to flee has already been sent, the fisher goes direct to the base of the brain, before the chicken even knows what hit it.)

Just as York was about to wind up his study last winter, he released the females in the woods behind his parents' place. The two circled and wrestled. One explored a stone wall. The other ran up and then down a tree. First one went off, then the other, bounding through the snow. That January, York saw lots of fisher tracks in those woods.

Holly's Holy Heritage

৯৯

For Woody Mills, every day is a holiday—or a holly day, to be exact.

As director of the Massachusetts Audubon Society's Ashumet Holly and Wildlife Sanctuary, he's responsible for tending more than a thousand holly trees and many dozens of holly bushes at the 49-acre sanctuary in East Falmouth.

December is especially hectic. For the past twenty-five years, Mills has spent the first half of the month harvesting sometimes up to twenty truckloads of the deep-green, berry-studded foliage. The first two weekends of the month, people flock to the sanctuary from miles around to put the "holly" in their holidays, buying swags, wreaths, and boughs to deck their halls.

Though old Christian legends say holly sprung up in the footsteps of Christ—its thorny leaves and blood-red berries foreshadowing His suffering—holly's role in winter celebrations is a tradition far older than Christmas. Long before there were any Christians to feed to the lions, ancient Romans sent boughs of holly, along with other gifts, to friends during the mid-December festival of Saturnalia, celebrating the god of agriculture. The ancient Celtic priests known as Druids also decorated with holly each winter, to make their homes more festive for visiting wood spirits.

And holly makes things more festive for more corporeal creatures, too. The plants provide important food and cover for wildlife, and have even served humans as medicine.

Today, holly is still revered for its startling beauty. "That intense, dark green, and the bright-red berries create such a vivid contrast that really shows up in a drab winter landscape," says Cheryl Lowe, horticulture director at the New England Wild Flower Society's Garden in the Woods in Framingham, Massachusetts. "No wonder people thought this was a sign of something important."

So close is the association between holly and holidays that the words share the same English root: holly, holy, and holiday all spring from "holi," the Middle English word for things associated with divine power. For centuries, the beautiful tree was considered magical and sacred in many areas of Europe. Pliny the Elder claimed that planting holly near a house or farm repelled poison and defended residents from lightning and witchcraft; a sprig of holly hung above your bed would ensure sweet dreams.

The 1st-century Roman scholar and naturalist also believed that the holly tree's tiny, May-blooming white flowers caused water to freeze, and that its hard, white wood possessed special powers as well: thrown at any animal, he wrote, a stick of holly wood would compel the creature to lie placidly down beside it.

Though some of these claims are fantastic, Pliny knew a thing or two: there is more to holly than meets the eye.

"People think of holly as a prickly-leafed, red-berry tree, and don't realize there are dozens and dozens of hollies," says Lieut. Col. Arthur E. Allen. But he certainly does: rooting in converted fish tanks at his home in Jamaica Plain, and growing on his 7-acre property in Rochester, Massachusetts, he has more than a hundred different kinds of holly: Chinese, Japanese, English, and American varieties, many of which he has obtained at meetings of the Holly Society of America, which he has attended in different cities over the past twelve years. "Some people collect coins, some people collect stamps; I collect hollies," he explains. "I enjoy holly trees because they're a neat tree—they don't make a mess in the fall. And they are one of the things that made our ancestors feel at home when they came to America."

Besides the familiar English holly tree and its similar-looking cousin, the slow-growing, long-lived American tree holly (which grows from Eastern Massachusetts to Florida and as far west as Oklahoma), there are more than four hundred other species of holly in the world, some of which don't look like holly at all. Though the family's name, *Aquifoliaceae,* means "needle leaf," not all hollies have spiny leaves, and not all are even evergreens.

Some hollies, such as the New England native we call winterberry or swamp holly, are low-growing shrubs that shed their spineless, oval leaves in winter. Some South American species are epiphytes, which begin their lives as vines, snake up trees, and then sever their connection with the ground, perching harmlessly on treetops.

And not all holly berries are red: some are yellow, orange, black, or white. According to Stephen Spongberg, director of the Polly Hill Arboretum in West Tisbury, Massachusetts, some of the low-growing, deciduous species native to Asia, as well as crosses between Asian and English species, are now very popular with gardeners and florists who make beautiful bouquets from the fruit-studded stems.

Those fruits are a blessing to wildlife. Though poisonous to humans (they make you throw up), the fruits of the American holly tree nourish forty-nine species of birds, including cedar waxwings, eastern bluebirds, flickers, turkeys, and robins. At the Ashumet Sanctuary, Mills often sees flocks of fifty to one hundred robins feasting among the trees' spiny foliage (which he says is fine with him as long as they leave some berries for his customers' boughs.) Deer, mice, and bears also relish the fruits.

Several of the nearly two dozen species of holly found in North America have provided medicines for Native Americans. The leaves were made into tonic teas to ease the symptoms of measles, cold, flu, pneumonia, pleurisy, and smallpox, and drops for sore eyes. They even used the poisonous berries in medicine, brewing a thick syrup to treat children's diarrhea.

In Germany, the leaves of another species were used as a substitute for tea, and yet another beverage, Paraguay Tea, is still drunk extensively in Brazil, prepared from the dried leaves and young shoots of another holly species that grows there. And in China, says botanist Shu-Ying Hu, holly is used widely in traditional medicine. In Hong Kong, the Chinese name of one species translates to "panacea."

All hollies contain an alkaloid called illicin, which taken in sufficient quantities acts as an emetic, laxative, and diuretic. It may not protect you against poison, but in the days before poison hotlines, if a person happened to have ingested poison, eating holly berries might help them evict it from their system.

Holly is worthy of our reverence, for it possesses its own kind of natural magic. While animals might not lie down beside a holly stick thrown at them, wildlife as well as domestic stock know a good thing when they see it. Wild animals hide in its thick cover and feast on its fruits. European rabbit breeders say their animals enjoy gnawing holly sticks placed in the hutch and that it stimulates appetite. European peasants used to feed the stems to cows, saying it helped produce sweet milk. And in the springtime, even insects love holly. At the Garden in the Woods, propogator and nursery manager Bill Cullina always finds the holly bushes' creamy-white flowers aswarm with honeybees, wasps, flower flies, and hover flies.

"Hollies have a special place in my heart," he says. Three decades ago, when he was a growing up in West Hartford, Connecticut, relatives sent his family four baby holly trees one Christmas. His family name, Cullina explains, means "Place of the Holly" in Gaelic. Now, in New England, the family has another place of the holly; the slow-growing trees are now four feet tall.

Ravens

Wolf-Birds of the Ancient Past

☙

They rode the shoulders of the Norse god, Odin. They were the hunting companions of the Indians. Even today, the Inuk Eskimos look to the big, glossy, black bird they call "Tulugaq" to tell them where the caribou are running.

For centuries, the wily, majestic raven has guided human endeavor. Ancient stories tell how ravens once lived among us, followed us into battle, hunted with us, and, in their deep, sonorous voices, told us their secrets. Circumpolar peoples believed ravens spoke to people, as well as to each other. That is why Odin sent a pair soaring from his shoulders each dawn to reconnoiter the ends of the earth. The raven saw all, and knew all. The Vikings believed a raven had discovered Iceland. The Koyukan Eskimos sought raven knowledge to heal sickness.

But today, to most of us, the raven is just a speck in the sky.

Or perhaps it's really a crow. "I think most people would not recognize a raven," says Bernd Heinrich, a University of Vermont biologist who has studied ravens for more than a decade; and even he admits, "I can't always tell myself."

With a practised eye, you can distinguish them. Ravens are three times as big as crows, and their tails are wedge-shaped, not square. Compare the flights of the two birds: crows flap more, while ravens glide on fluid wingbeats.

The best clue, though, is that crows, who are in the same

family as ravens, are easy to find at roadsides, often in family groups, picking at a road kill, or at parks, raiding garbage. The raven is more likely to feed on winter-killed deer and moose in forests. In late winter and early spring, as thawing snows reveal a bonanza of winter-killed meat, ravens are building their stick nests in deep pine forests and along cliffs.

The raven is larger, wilder, and more carnivorous than the crow—which is why ravens are also rarer. Fifty years ago, you probably couldn't have found one. Because they eat meat, ravens were blamed for killing sheep and lambs, and relentlessly poisoned and shot. By 1900, they were largely exterminated in most of the east and midwest.

Now, as farms retreat and forests regrow, ravens are returning. In some areas of the U.S. and Europe, ravens have even returned to cities, nesting on churches in downtown Zurich, and are as common as pigeons in Yukon towns. They are now found all over Vermont, Maine, and New Hampshire and in the wilder areas of Massachusetts. Their numbers are still steadily growing.

But now that they are back, we have forgotten who they are.

Happily, watching wild ravens near a remote cabin in Maine and observing captive and formerly captive ravens near his home in Vermont, Bernd Heinrich is rediscovering what ravens have to tell us. Those black specks in the sky are lives breathtakingly rich, complex, and individual.

"I'm learning new things all the time!" Heinrich said in an interview. The spacious aviary where he studies captive ravens is the stage for dramas as rich as a human soap opera. "Just yesterday," he said, "I almost witnessed a murder." The six birds who live there had been together for two years, and had established a dominance hierarchy. Two had paired off: their names are Red and Blue, and they were clearly in the mood for nesting. As a result, they didn't want the others to invade their space, and they ganged up on neighbors White, Green, and Yellow. And they nearly killed Yellow. But it was the behavior of Yellow's friend, Orange, that astouded Heinrich. Once Red began the assault on Yellow, the others joined in—except Orange. Orange perched aside, vibrating his tail—a gesture usually thought to be an invitation to mate. But in this case, said Heinrich, the gesture was perhaps an entreaty: "Please, please, don't kill this bird." He rescued the bird. "Otherwise," said Heinrich, "they would have killed her for sure."

Though birds are more closely related to dinosaurs than to humans, ravens seem, in their complexity, intelligence, and behavioral flexibility, like our avian twins.

"There is something unique about ravens that permits or encourages an uncanny closeness to develop with humans," Heinrich writes in *The Mind of the Raven*, his second book devoted to the species. And that may well be because we are so much alike.

Like us, ravens form devoted couples and will mate for life, which can last forty years or longer. Like us, they share food and information—and their altruism extends beyond their own family. Like us, to ravens, communication is crucial. Their voices can carry a mile. As early as 1903, ornithologist Thomas Nutall claimed to have identified sixty-four different raven calls. Heinrich says that like in human language, ravens seem to possess different dialects in different areas. And ravens' behavior varies widely from group to group, from place to place, as it does with groups of humans. "I'm pretty sure," he asserts, "it's culture."

Culture outside of humankind is a controversial idea. But if anyone is qualified to make such a statement about ravens, it's Heinrich. He has spent more than fifteen seasons in the field observing ravens in the wild. Because they have been so persecuted, they are extraordinarily difficult to study. But Heinrich is an extraordinary researcher—by age ten he had already lived for six years in the woods as a refugee in a northern German forest—and prepared to go to extraordinary lengths. On and off for more than a dozen field seasons, he has lived on the edge of Mount Blue State Park in western Maine in a tarpaper shack—a cabin he kept unheated during the day for his first two years of fieldwork, to avoid alarming the shy birds with chimney smoke.

He courted these wild ravens with meat, their favorite food.

Like a suitor brings his beloved flowers and candy, he scoured
roads and farms for road kills and carcasses for his birds. One
time he procured a slaughtered Holstein in Vermont, and then
drove the four hours to Maine with its carcass packed around
him in the jeep, the hoofed legs sticking out the windows. While
researching the birds' behavior for his book, *Ravens in Winter*, he
estimates he brought the ravens more than eight tons of meat—
bait he then dutifully protected by urinating near it, to repel coyotes who might steal it from his birds.

Meat is central to the story of these birds—just as anthropol-
ogists believe that meat is central to the story of humanity. A
raven, writes Heinrich, will eat "all the dead animals it can find,
and all the live ones it can kill." As he reported in *Ravens in
Winter*, young ravens give a particular call to alert other ravens
to a meat bonanza in the woods. By sharing their knowledge,
these young birds cement friendships with other ravens—an
arrangement, he notes, like the meat-sharing system of the Kala-
hari Bushmen, who distribute all large game among the group to
reinforce alliances.

To find meat, ravens also follow predators—polar bears,
grizzly bears, wolves—and people.

As part of his research for *The Mind of the Raven*, Heinrich
traveled to Yellowstone National Park. After wolves were re-in-
troduced to the park in 1994, rangers noticed that ravens immediately began to travel with them, and that the birds were always
present at kills. It's an observation wolf researchers have noted
for decades. Heinrich calls them "wolf-birds." When hunting
wolves pause, researchers note, the accompanying ravens harass
them, urging them on. Ravens not only travel with predators;
they may also help them, serving the wolves as extra eyes and
ears to alert their mammalian companions to both opportunity
and danger.

Once, believes Henrich, humans had the wolf's-eye view of
these majestic and mysterious birds. "I think they were closely
associated with humans the way they are now associated with
wolves," he said in an interview. "Ravens associated with the best
predators." Ravens still follow moose hunters in Maine and deer

hunters in the Scottish highlands, as they used to follow Vikings into battle. For in both instances, the ravens knew that hunters and warriors would lead them to meat.

Sometimes ravens even seem to take the lead. On Baffin Island, just west of Greenland and north of Hudson Bay, Inuit hunters called ravens to ask them to lead them to polar bears and caribou. The raven, they said, would give a musical gong-like note three times, and then tumble from the sky in the direction of the game. "They believed in the raven strongly, and followed it," Inuit hunter Abe Opik told Heinrich, "And after they killed the caribou or the polar bear, they always left the raven the choicest tidbits of meat as a reward." Two fellow meat-eaters—human and raven—depended on one another.

But today, over much of the circumpolar world where ravens still soar, the intimacy we once shared with these great birds has been shattered. When people switched from a hunting lifestyle to farming, ravens no longer followed our kind. And when we began to poison and shoot them, they learned to avoid us assiduously. Their culture, Heinrich would say, changed as ours did.

And yet our mutual capacity for closeness remains. People who have adopted sick or orphaned ravens have forged devoted and demanding relationships with birds whose intellect has repeatedly startled them. Konrad Lorenz, founder of the modern study of animal behavior, had a pet raven he named Roah, whose inventive reasoning proved perplexing. One day Roah brought Lorenz some wet laundry that had fallen off the line. Lorenz rewarded him with food. Thereafter, Roah raided laundry lines far and wide, hoping to please the scientist by showering him with gifts of his neighbors' wet underwear.

Heinrich, too, has raised pet ravens, and advises the task is not for the faint of heart—or for those who prefer furniture, carpeting, and drapes unstreaked by raven feces and unshredded by inquisitive beaks. (However, he did meet a tame raven, Jacob, who lived harmlessly among priceless art and antiques in an apartment he shared with a doctor in Oberhausen, Germany. For some reason, Jacob reserved his destructive urges for the doctor's junk mail.)

Another tame raven, Merlin, lived with a California couple and regularly flew free outdoors. With a unique, two-note whistle, Merlin would alert his human companions to scenes or events he considered important. One day, when the man was sitting on a hillside, Merlin returned from his usual explorations with an urgent message. He perched on his companion, pecked his face and pulled his collar; he then flew a loop down the valley, came back and repeated the entire procedure. The man got up and followed.

There he found a bobcat that had just killed a ground squirrel. Re-enacting legends thousands of generations old, Merlin had directed his human companion to meat.

It's no wonder, says Heinrich, that ravens hold such a prominent place in our myths and legends; and it's no wonder they can still powerfully stir our hearts today. "Ravens are, and likely always have been, not just wolf-birds," writes Heinrich. "They are our birds as well."

Ermine

Concentrated Carnivore

๛

*E*rin Sokol is now a lawyer in Washington, D.C., but the image of what she saw one Christmas as a child remains as vivid as an electric shock.

Sokol and her stepmother were seated on a bench in their New Hampshire kitchen, looking out on a four-foot-high snowbank pushed up against the sliding glass door. Suddenly a tiny face appeared in the middle of the snow.

The bright black eyes and dark nose stood out against the creature's white fur. Even though the face was only an inch wide, and seen across the room, the animal's gaze was fierce, so intense that they grabbed each other and gasped.

And then, in a flash, the weasel vanished, leaving a translucent tunnel behind.

Todd Fuller, now a biology professor at the University of Massachusetts at Amherst, had a similar experience—one that can only be described as a visitation. He was a graduate student, living in a cabin while studying wolves and caribou in Alberta, Canada one winter. The cabin's old woodstove was burning too hot, so he opened the door. "And in came a little weasel," he said. "A little white, curious creature stuck its head around the door to see what was up. It looked around and scooted around the cabin. And then it left."

Other than the trimming on Santa Claus's coat, most of us rarely get a glimpse of an ermine. They are not particularly abundant (one weasel per three acres is considered high density) and their numbers fluctuate wildly depending on their rodent prey. Weasels are solitary animals, who keep in touch with other weasels only by scent messages left in their scats. But these intense little carnivores—weasels dressed in their white winter coats—are living throughout New England's wild, rural, and even some suburban areas. Many of us have passed their tiny tracks in the snow, mistaking them for those of mice or even birds. Only occasionally do these fierce little predators burst directly into our lives—and when they do, they leave us breathless with wonder.

They seem far too bold for their size. Paul Rezendes, a Massachusetts-based tracker and author of *The Wild Within*, once watched mesmerized as an ermine not much longer than his finger walked up to him—a monster more than a thousand times its size—and fearlessly began to investigate his backpack. Rezendes was in a wet meadow full of purple joe pye weed in Royalston, Massachusetts, and had just set down his photography equipment in a small clearing he had created. "This animal was close enough I could reach out and touch it," he said. "He jumped up on my pack and sniffed my photography gear. And he did this three times. I am willing to bet that ermine had never seen a human being. And I was something totally alien—but he wasn't afraid."

These weasels are pure, concentrated carnivore. "There is something enormously satisfactory about a weasel," writes New Zealand researcher Carolyn King in her book, *The Natural History of Weasels and Stoats*. "It has the perfection, grace, and efficiency of a well-designed tool in the hands of an expert."

"The fierceness of the family is fascinating," agrees Steve Sheffield, a wildlife biologist with the U.S. Fish and Wildlife Service in Arlington, Virginia. All three of New England's weasel species are smaller than some of the prey they hunt. (The least weasel, the long-tailed, and the short-tailed weasel are brown with white bellies in summer, and in New England they turn white in the winter. All three are called ermine, at least in some quarters, when in winter pelage.) The smallest species, the least weasel, is only as long as a man's finger, and weighs 30–65 grams, about as much as a vole. It's the world's smallest carnivore, Sheffield points out. And yet all three weasel species are capable of feats no lion could perform.

With short legs and a tube shaped body, a weasel can follow a vole or lemming into the tightest quarters (which it will sometimes claim as its own, evicting the previous tenant by eating it, and then lining the bedchamber with the fur). It can hunt beneath the snow. It can swim, climb trees, and leap into the air to kill a bird as it takes flight. With vise-like jaws, it can bring down an animal twice its own size, kill it with a single bite to the neck, and carry it off at a bounding run.

Weasels are fierce because they have to be. "Every meal is so valuable to them, so critical," says Roger Powell, an associate professor of zoology at North Carolina State University, who has studied weasels for more than three decades. To feed a galloping pulse—a short-tailed weasel's heart beats 360–390 times a minute—a captive weasel needs to consume a quarter to a third of its body weight each day. In the wild, they need much more: five to ten meals a day. "We were going through mice like crazy," Powell says, remembering the time he shared his home with six weasels of three species.

Small mammals spend more energy maintaining their body temperature than large mammals, because of their relatively larger surface area. With their long, thin shape, weasels have even more surface area than other critters—three times that of a lemming of the same weight. And they can't afford to store energy in the form of fat. They have to stay lithe so they can slip through vole tunnels. Instead, they kill everything they can at every opportunity, and store the excess for later consumption.

This wise evolutionary strategy can lead to tragedy if a weasel gets in the hen house. The poultryman who finds his entire flock dead (and often headless) may consider weasels wasteful, vicious animals. What he does not realize, says Powell, is that weasels never evolved to deal with the superabundance of a hen house, but as vole specialists hunting Pleistocene tundras. (And the weasel would certainly come back to eat those hens, but usually by the time it does, the farmer has already carted them away.) King's reviews of studies of weasels show that many farmers should be grateful for weasels' appetites, for they help efficiently protect grain stores from the depredations of mice and voles.

Hunting weasels tailor their methods to changing targets and opportunities. Tiny, zigzagging five-toed tracks in the snow illustrate the technique: bounding here and there, investigating every patch of cover, searching every hole, an ermine seeks out its prey, writes King, "with restless energy and fierce concentration." They often stand on their hind legs to listen, a posture the Germans call "macht mannchen"—"making a little man." In deeper snow, you may also see where an ermine dove beneath the snow and tunneled, creating surface bulges like that of a mole in dirt. A weasel may cover a mile in just a few hours of hunting.

In addition to always worrying about where the next meal is coming from, weasels have another pressing problem: avoiding becoming a meal themselves. Unlike larger carnivores, these predators are often themselves prey. Any predator who eats a weasel, Powell points out, scores two points: it gets a meal and eliminates a competitor. Other predators are the reason weasels' coats turn white in the winter in snowy climes. This camouflage helps protect them from hunting owls, hawks, coyotes, foxes, bobcats, as well as dogs and cats.

Unfortunately, that luxurious white fur attracts human predators, too. Ancient American Indians used ermine skins to trim the ceremonial clothes of chiefs, and the white winter coat of weasels still adorns the cloaks of British justices. Though today's market for their fur is small, in 1937, 50,000 ermine skins were sent from Canada just to adorn the robes of celebrants for the coronation of King George VI—a wave of slaughter that makes a weasel's night in a henhouse seem as benign as a housewife in a grocery store.

Far from being bloodthirsty killers, weasels are "downright sweet" if you get to know them, says Powell. In her book, King quotes Englishman, P. Drabble, who described his captive weasel, Teasy, as "a sprite—a golden leaf on the tongue of a whirlwind."

The playful little animal bowled around the living room "like a tiny inflated rubber tyre—his cartwheeling twisted this way and that over the carpet and up on to the settee beside me. I always knew what his next act would be," Drabble wrote. "From the cover of his dynamic camouflage, he would dive on to my fingertip with mock ferocity, but in reality as gently as a kitten— then he'd gradually relax, until he was licking the tips of my fingers and croon his high-pitched little purring love-song."

One of Powell's long-tailed weasels gave birth to two kits in his house. One of the babies was so affectionate she would curl up in the biologist's hand. It was a magical feeling, he said, and an honor few humans experience. "Holding one in your hand," he said, "is like holding electricity."

Of Mice, Moths, and Men

❦

*E*leanor Briggs was in her New Hampshire kitchen making madelines when she heard the mouse trap snap.

She put the pastries in the oven and went to investigate. The mouse was dead all right—but it was still moving. A wound near its groin indicated that something was still alive beneath the mouse's skin. It was an inch-and-a-half-long maggot. Yuck! She flung the mouse, maggot and all, behind a smokebush in the side yard. But out of sight was not out of mind. Briggs, a careful observer of nature, had never seen anything like this; she thought such an odd sight might be significant.

And she was right. In the trap in her kitchen that evening, she had glimpsed part of a story as rich in character and plot as a Russian novel: a tale of mice, maggots, moths, and men, involving two diseases, one summertime drought, several foreign invasions, and decades of scientific sleuthing.

And while no one knows for sure, such signs may act as portents: such sights can foretell a leafless summer, months away.

This is a story of surprising connections between ordinary creatures in our woods, fields, and yards, and how their interactions and natural cycles can profoundly affect our lives, from autumn roadkills to summer shade.

The tale begins as tall oaks do: with acorns. And it could well end as some oaks do: with gypsy moths. The mouse and the maggot are intricately tied to both.

Acorns provide crucial food for 150 species of birds and mammals, making up a full 25 percent of the diets of black bears, raccoons, gray squirrels, and wild turkeys. But for white footed mice, acorns are particularly important.

"Acorns drive their numbers," says Bill Healy, wildlife biologist with the U.S. Forest Service at the North East Research Station in Amherst, Massachusetts. "Acorns alone account for 60 percent of the variation in mouse numbers from year to year."

In good acorn years, there are lots of mice. When acorns are few, the mouse population declines within months.

Mouse numbers can vary immensely, as Jeff Boettner can attest. A researcher at the University of Massachusetts at Amherst, he has live-trapped and tagged perhaps 35,000 mice over the past fourteen years. Working at two different study sites, on Cape Cod and at the Quabbin Reservoir, he found as few as two mice per hectare the autumn Briggs' madeline baking was interrupted—in areas that, in the previous year, supported a hundred. Come spring, he said, there would be fewer still—because of a summer drought, and two bad acorn years in a row. And then, there's the matter of the botflies.

These interesting insects, which look like enormous houseflies, have a fascinating life history, including a mating ritual in which the male flies gather from miles around at a historic "lekking" ground to attract females. The adult fly has a gorgeous face, with black freckles on a white background, sort of like a bald-faced hornet. But these fine attributes are lost on the white-footed mouse, to whom botflies are misery incarnate.

The flies lay their eggs in July at the entrance to mouse burrows. An unlucky mouse may bush against them and ingest some while grooming its fur. The eggs hatch, and each at-first tiny maggot tries to migrate to the mouse's groin—where it can grow to an inch-and-a-half long, creating a wound in the mouse's skin through which the maggot breathes. When ready to exit, it pops out of the hole and pupates, to hatch out as an adult fly in June.

Happily for us, these botflies don't infest people (there are some in the tropics that do).

"This is a really bad year," said Boettner. Briggs' mouse was far from rare: some mice he had trapped had as many as eight giant maggots in them. And while they seldom kill their host—the wound heals completely within a few days—the baby flies are an enormous drain on their host during the fifteen days or so they are maturing. Even one of the giant parasites could slow down a mouse enough to make the difference between escaping from a predator or falling prey, or surviving the winter in good enough health to produce a large litter in the spring. The mouse population, Boettner said, was in for a crash.

Fewer mice in the spring? Many folks might think that's just fine. But among the biggest advocates of fewer mice are some of the East's most destructive pests: the leaf-munching larvae of the gypsy moth, for whom white-footed mice are Public Enemy Number One.

Gypsy moths are foreign interlopers, aliens from Europe and Asia. They were purposely imported to Melrose, Massachusetts in 1868 as part of a hare-brained scheme to interbreed them with silk moths (impossible, as they are unrelated species). The insects escaped from captivity, invaded nearby forests, and have been spreading ever since. Today they threaten oak and aspen forests as far away as North Carolina, West Virginia, and Michigan.

Unlike the relatively harmless tent-making fall webworms, with whom gypsy moth caterpillars are often confused, these caterpillars can defoliate entire forests. During an outbreak "in June and July, it looks like winter,"said Dr. Joseph Elkinton, an expert on the pests and a professor of entomology at the University of Massachusetts, Amherst. "There's nothing left."

Although the caterpillars prefer oaks to other species, during an outbreak they'll even eat the needles off hemlocks, he said. Many of the defoliated trees eventually die from the stress. And outbreaks can continue for one, two, even three or more years in a row.

So we ought to be grateful for the appetites of white-footed mice.

They are among the few animals who eat the caterpillars. For one thing, the caterpillars are active only at night, when few birds are hunting. For another, the larvae are covered with prickly, distasteful hairs. But the nocturnal white-footed mouse has found a solution: the dexterous rodent simply strips away the caterpillars' prickly coating like a person peels a banana.

So important are white-footed mice as predators of gypsy moth larvae that when mouse populations rise, gypsy moth populations fall. That's one reason Boettner counts mouse numbers each year. Foresters, landowners, and ecologists welcome any clue to predicting when gypsy moth outbreaks are most likely to occur.

The last serious outbreak in New England occurred in 1982. It was the worst defoliation of the century. "It stripped the woods of Massachusetts bare," remembers Healy.

Then in 1989, Healy and colleagues were bracing for another outbreak. All the signs were present: there had been two poor acorn years in succession. Mouse numbers were down. That spring, there were gypsy moth caterpillars everywhere. But then, before they had caused any serious damage, they started to drop dead.

Nobody knew what was happening. "Gypsy moths were here about one hundred years, and when we finally figured out what was going on," said Healy, "something new happened."

It turned out the caterpillars that summer fell victim to another disease, one caused by a fungus. The fungus, like the moths themselves, was a foreigner, but it was an invited one: it had been purposely introduced to Cape Cod soils from Japan in the earlier part of the century to control the moths. But it had inexplicably vanished. Now, equally inexplicably, it was back. And foresters were delighted to have another control agent in the arsenal against the hated caterpillars. Their other major weapon was a virus. The fungus could prevent the outbreak, while the virus could only terminate it.

But in nature, nothing's a sure thing. Fungus needs moisture to thrive. A drought—one that stresses trees and is likely to starve mice—can also kill the fungus. And the picture could be more complex than we can imagine. There could be other players in the drama, creatures with their own cycles, that we haven't yet observed or understood. "Perhaps, between the mice and the virus and the fungus, and some other parasites, they will reach equilibrium here," says Healy.

It may have already happened. As it turned out, the summer after the maggoty mice, there was no massive outbreak of gypsy moths. And nobody knows why.

In western Europe, where the gypsy moths evolved, they seldom overpopulate into tree-destroying outbreaks. They have had centuries to adapt to the intricate cycles of animals, diseases, trees, and weather whose interactions form their habitat and ours.

Animals That Aren't?

⠀

ॐ

*M*aureen Clark was carving a ham on Christmas Eve
morning, when her sixteen-year-old nephew, Rory
Grant, glanced out the kitchen window and saw something really big moving in the back yard.

"What is that?" he asked.

Some pretty impressive wildlife wanders through Clark's
Lincoln, New Hampshire yard—coyotes, bears, and, the week
before, a big bull moose. But she'd never seen anything like this:
Grant estimated it was 24 inches high, 80–100 pounds, tawny
with a long tail. It was about 35 feet away, and partly obscured
by a big rock.

"We were mesmerized by it," said Clark. "I was just thinking, Wow, there is a big cat out in my back yard!" Then the
sharp-witted photographer rushed to get her video camera. But
by the time she got to the window, the animal had moved further
away, into beech saplings and brush.

For many hours over the course of several days, eight New
Hampshire Fish and Game wildlife biologists viewed the three
seconds of Clark's videotape showing the animal. Was it a mountain lion—an animal supposedly extinct in New Hampshire
since the turn of the century? In some frames the tail looked as if
were striped, like a house cat's. In others, the ears seemed too
pointy for a cat—more like a coyote's.

Their verdict: "We can confidently say," states Fish and

Game spokesman Eric Aldrich, "that it's inconclusive."

Only one thing's for certain: "It's remarkable how difficult it is to tell what you're looking at out there," says Tom French at the Massachusetts Division of Fisheries and Wildlife's Natural Heritage and Endangered Species Program.

An animal's color and shape seem to change with back lighting or glare; branches and brush can obscure it. Even if you get a clear look at an animal, say, in an open field, it can be terribly hard to gauge its size. And without all this information, it's often impossible to tell for sure what you've seen—or to help others identify it for you.

Even the experts are sometimes confused. Tufts veterinary clinic's Mark Pokras, an assistant professor of wildlife medicine, and wildlife biologists Bill Davis and Tom French were working on the bald eagle re-introduction project at the Quabbin Reservoir one morning ten years ago when a tawny flash slipped across the road only yards in front of their Jeep. "I am convinced it's a cougar—100 percent," thought Pokras. "I am positive. I am absolutely sure. We really have to track this thing down."

The biologists leapt from the vehicle to follow the animal.

"So we were walking through the woods along the trail of mashed down ferns and brush and climb the top of a rise," the biologist continued, "and standing there was an immature coyote." It had a long thin tail, and was standing in the yellowish, dawn light.

Then he looked at the tracks: they were too small to be a mountain lion's, only one-and-a-half inches across. And the tracks showed toenails, seldom seen in cat tracks but almost always a clue to a dog's. "I was mightily chagrined."

In the woods, things are not always what they seem. Sometimes they are even stranger.

Take for instance, the big bird of prey that birders kept reporting in a farmer's field in Middleboro, Massachusetts one recent winter. It turned out it was a caracara—a wide-winged fishing eagle native to the subtropics of Texas and Florida and tropical South America. No one knows how it got there.

And the caracara's not the only tropical visitor to New

England that winter. Wildlife officials got a call about a porcupine hit on Route 6A in Barnstable—an area where porcupines are not normally found. It turned out the injured animal was even further from its normal range than previously thought: the veterinarian identified it as an African crested porcupine. It had escaped from a zoo.

At least twelve people reported seeing a two-and-a-half-foot-high, kangaroo-like creature hopping through the streets of Concord, Acton, and Foxboro—several continents beyond its normal range in Australia. Another one visited Malden, Melrose, Medford, Stoneham, and Winchester. It was a Bennett's wallaby named Aardu, who had escaped from the Stoneham Zoo. No one ever figured out where the other missing marsupial came from. Strange as it sounds, it may have been an escaped pet—which accounts for the wandering 50-pound Asian jungle cat, the strolling African serval, and a handful of mountain lions that Fish and Wildlife have picked up around Massachusetts over the past ten years.

The flamingo on Lake Champlain was probably another story, though. Vermont authorities said the bird likely blew in from Florida during a summer storm in 1980.

Some animal sightings aren't animals at all. In a small midwestern town several years ago, folks got so worried about a black bear they saw marooned on top of a telephone pole that the townspeople eventually cut the telephone pole down. To the chagrin of the concerned citizens, when the pole came down they found they had "rescued" a black garbage bag.

That's Pokras' favorite story of misidentification—partly because he made the opposite mistake himself several years ago. He was looking for birds at a small county park south of Houston, along the banks of a little river disappointingly filled with trash. There was even a big piece of black plastic lodged in one of the dead trees. He came within three feet of it when he realized it wasn't a plastic trash bag, but a black vulture. "And I didn't even notice it was alive!"

That many reports of exotic animals turn out to be cases of mistaken identity is lucky indeed—at least, for those of us who would rather live in New England than in some *National Geographic* special. If all the weird critter calls wildlife officials answer were correct, you couldn't walk out of your house without tripping over wolves and wolverines, badgers and armadillos, and you'd need an umbrella to protect yourself from all the bald eagles falling out of the sky.

Wildlife agencies, veterinarians, and Audubon societies get these calls every day. "I call them 'The Animals That Aren't,'" says Eric Orff, a wildlife biologist with the New Hampshire Fish and Game Department. For twenty-two years, like his counterparts across the country, he's has been fielding calls like these:

"A 160-pound wolf is lurking at the edge of the woods!" Wolves were exterminated from New England a century ago. But even if they were making a comeback—which biologists insist hasn't yet happened—there couldn't be enough to account for all the calls Orff gets in New Hampshire reporting their presence—usually one a week. But there are plenty of coyotes—and dogs.

"I have a bald eagle in my yard!" A Cape Cod woman who called the Massachusetts Department of Fisheries and Wildlife described the bird to a tee: it had a big white head, a big curved yellow beak, and black body. Careful questioning revealed the bird also had webbed feet, and was actually a black-backed sea gull.

Although eagles are returning to New England, often the "eagle" sighting turns out to be another, more common bird of prey—a kestrel or hawk. But even these birds are often misidentified. One man reported finding an injured peregrine falcon and brought it to Tufts' veterinary clinic. It was a baby pigeon.

"A bloodthirsty fisher is ripping the guts out of everything in the neighborhood." Fishers, sleek members of the weasel family, are seldom seen but often blamed for imagined, wanton destruction. Usually folks who call Orff about fishers didn't, as it turns out, actually see anything, but they heard something—often an eerie scream in the night (which might be a tomcat or a fox).

When folks do see a fisher, which weighs about seven pounds, they sometimes report a wolverine—a heavily built,

70-pound carnivore that lives in the wilderness of northern Maine and out west.

Such dramatic increases in size aren't infrequent. Twenty-pound coyotes morph into 160-pound wolves, and 10-pound house cats grow into 100-pound mountain lions. Some of this has to do with perspective. "We are a lousy judge of distance," says Jim Hall, hunter education coordinator at New Hampshire Fish and Wildlife. In re-training hunters to shoot steel shot instead of lead bullets to protect waterways from lead poisoning several years ago, he found that most hunters said that a nine-foot-wide target crossbar looked to them like it was six feet wide. "Most people underestimate distance," he said.

But another reason animals may appear larger than they are is that their wildness looms large in our imagination. And this can profoundly affect what we see.

"Partly you see what's there," says Pokras, "and partly you see what you expect." Or want. Or fear. It's said that seeing is believing, but the opposite is sometimes truer: sometimes we see what we believe.

Philosophers and naturalists have known for centuries that we don't just see with our eyes. "The mind's eye is not passive," Amherst College physics professor Arthur Zajonc writes in his book *Catching the Light: The Entwined History of Light and Mind*. Five hundred years before Christ, the physician, statesman, and poet Empedocles theorized that a sort of fire burned in the human eye like a lantern, and that sight was cast like a ray from the seer to the thing seen. Euclid, the great Alexandrian mathematician, believed this, too, as did Plato.

In a way, they were right. Belief in a "fire in the eye" was quenched by the mid-1900s, but psychologists are still exploring what Zajonc calls "the inner, psychological pole of sight." Investigations of hunting accidents reveal that, though rarely, sometimes people have honestly "seen" and fired upon a buck—only to find they have shot a person. Psychologists call this phenomenon "premature closure" or "early blur": the seer glimpses an outline or a shadow and psychologically fills in the missing parts. After waiting in a blind for hours for a wild turkey to appear, the first big thing that moves may well look to the hunter's eyes like a wild turkey. (Hunter orange, notes Hall, works well because it interrupts premature closure, acting as a "circuit breaker.") Premature closure can turn a house cat into a mountain lion, a dog into a wolf, or a seagull into an eagle.

How, then, can you ever find out what you've really seen out your window? Wildlife experts offer this advice:

Note the important features of the creature: its color, shape of beak or ears or tail, color of fur or feathers. Photograph or videotape the animal if possible; if not, write down the description as you are looking at it.

Try to gauge size by noting its height relative to a bush, tree, rock, or stalk. If you have a videotape, after the animal has left, have someone videotape you at the site the animal was standing for perspective.

Look for tracks or scat the animal has left behind. Photograph or videotape these with a ruler in the picture. Protect the evidence beneath an overturned bucket until an expert can help you identify it.

Call state fish and wildlife officials as soon as possible. Your sighting may be important. Your evidence could help document the existence or return of a rare species, or you might have discovered an escaped captive, like the wandering wallaby, who needs your help.

Everyone who's looked at Maureen Clark's videotape agrees she did everything right—and still no one knows for sure what she saw. For sometimes mystery is the essence of nature. So keep looking out the window. You never know what you might see.

Selected Bibliography

Mammals

Goodridge, Harry and Lew Dietz. *A Seal Called Andre*. Camden, Me.: Down East Books, 1975.

Gorman, Martyn L. and Stone, David R. *The Natural History of Moles*. Ithaca, NY: Cornell University Press, 1990.

King, Carolyn. *The Natural History of Weasels and Stoats*. London: Christopher Helm, 1989.

Kinkead, Eugene. *Squirrel Book*. New York: EP Dutton, 1980.

Langford, Cameron. *The Winter of the Fisher*. New York: Norton, 1971.

Mellanby, Kenneth. *The Mole*. London: Collins, 1971.

Nowak, Ronald M. and Paradiso, John L., editors. *Walker's Mammals of the World*, 4th Edition, Volumes I and II. Baltimore: Johns Hopkins Press, 1983.

Rue, Leonard Lee III. *The Deer of North America*. New York: The Lyons Press, 1997.

Ryden, Hope. *God's Dog: The North American Coyote*. New York: Coward, McCann, and Geoghegan, 1975.

Stokes, Don and Lillian. *A Guide to Animal Tracking and Behavior*. Boston: Little, Brown, 1986.

Thomas, Elizabeth Marshall. *The Hidden Life of Dogs*. Boston: Houghton Mifflin, 1993.

Wishner, Lawrence. *Eastern Chipmunks: Secrets of their Solitary Lives*. Washington DC: Smithsonian Press, 1982.

Plants

Bland, John H. *Forests of Lilliput: The Realm of Mosses and Lichens*. Englewood Cliffs, NJ: Prentice-Hall, 1971.

Darwin, Charles. *Insectivorous Plants*. London: John Murray, 1875.

Dwelley, Marilyn J. *Summer and Fall Wildflowers of New England*. Camden, Me.: Down East Books, 1977.

Elias, Thomas S. and Dykeman, Peter A. *Field Guide to North American Edible Wild Plants*. New York: Van Nostrand Reinhold Company, 1982.

Going, Maud. *With the Trees*. New York: Baker and Taylor, 1905.

Kavasch, E. Barrie. *Enduring Harvests*. Old Saybrook, Conn.: Globe Pequot Press, 1995.

Sanders, Jack. *Hedgemaids and Fairy Candles: The Lives and Lore of North American Wildflowers*. Camden, Me: Ragged Mountain Press, 1993.

Soule, Deb. *The Roots of Healing*. Secacus, NJ: Carol Publishing Group, 1995.

Stein, Sarah. *Planting Noah's Garden*. Boston: Houghton Mifflin, 1997.

Stirling, Dorothy. *The Story of Mosses, Ferns and Mushrooms*. New York: Doubleday, 1955.

Sumner, Judith. *The Natural History of Medicinal Plants*. Portland, Or.: Timber Press, 2000.

Wallner, Jeff and DiGregorio, Mario. *New England's Mountain Flowers: A High Country Heritage*. Missoula, Montana: Mountain Press Publishing Co., 1997.

Birds

Bodio, Stephen J. *Aloft*. New York: Lyons and Burford Publishers, 1990.

Clark, Neal. *Birds on the Move: A Guide to New England's Avian Invaders*. Unity, Me.: North Country Press, 1988.

Forbush, Edward Howe. *A Natural History of American Birds*. Boston: Houghton Mifflin, 1925.

Heinrich, Bernd. *The Mind of the Raven*. New York: Cliff Street Books, 1999.

———. *Ravens in Winter*. New York: Simon and Schuster, 1989.

Kaufman, Kenn. *Lives of North American Birds*. Boston: Houghton Mifflin, 1996.

Kilham, Lawrence. *On Watching Birds*. Chelsea, Vt.: Chelsea Green, 1988.

———. *The American Crow and The Common Raven*. College Station, Tx.: Texas A&M University Press, 1989.

Stokes, Donald and Lillian. *A Guide to Bird Behavior*. Volumes I
    and II. Boston: Little, Brown and Company, 1983.
Wiberg, Hugh. *Hand-Feeding Wild Birds*. Pownal, Vt.: Storey
    Books, Annedawn Publishing, 1999.

Insects

Brewer, Jo and Winter, Dave. *Butterflies and Moths: A Companion
    to Your Field Guide*. New York: Prentice Hall, 1986.
Buchmann, Stephen L. and Nabhan, Gary Paul. *The Forgotten
    Pollinators*. Washington DC: Island Press, 1996.
Dixon, Royal and Eddy, Brayton. *Personality of Insects*. New
    York: Henry Holt, 1924.
Evans, Arthur V. and Bellamy, Charles L. *An Inordinate Fondness
    for Beetles*. New York: Henry Holt and Company, Inc. 1996.
Holland, W.J. *The Moth Book*. New York: Doubleday, 1903.
Pyle, Robert Michael. *Chasing Monarchs: Migrating with the
    Butterflies of Passage*. Boston: Houghton Mifflin, 1999.
Sargent, Theodore. *Legion of Night: The Underwing Moths*.
    Amherst, Ma: University of Massachusetts Press, 1976.
Stokes, Donald. *A Guide to Observing Insect Lives*. Boston: Little,
    Brown and Company, 1983.
Winter, Dave. *Butterfly Gardening*. The Xerces Society with the
    Smithsonian Institution. San Francisco: Sierra Club
    Books/Washington DC: National Wildlife Federation, 1990.

Geology

Allport, Susan. *Sermons in Stone*. New York: W. W. Norton,
    1990.
Eckert, Alan W. *The Northeastern Quadrant*. New York: Harper
    & Row, 1987.
Raymo, Chet and Maureen E. *Written in Stone: A Geological
    History of the United States*. Chester, Ct.: Globe Pequot
    Press, 1989.
Roberts, David D. *A Field Guide to Geology: Eastern North
    America*. Boston: Houghton Mifflin (Peterson Field Guides)
    1996.

Trefil, James S. *A Scientist at the Seashore*. New York: Macmillan, 1984.

Wessels, Tom. *The Granite Landscape: A Natural History of America's Mountain Domes, from Acadia to Yosemite*. Woodstock, Vt.: Countryman Press, 2001.

Aquatic and Marine Creatures

Carroll, David M. *The Year of the Turtle: A Natural History*. Charlotte, Vt: Camden House Publishing, 1991.

———, *Swampwalker's Journal*. Boston: Houghton Mifflin, 1999.

Carson, Rachel. *The Edge of the Sea*. Boston: Houghton Mifflin, 1955.

Morgan, Ann Haven. *Field Book of Ponds and Streams*. New York: Putnam, 1930.

Essays

Anderson, Charles R., Editor. *Thoreau's World: Miniatures from His Journal*. New York: Prentice Hall, 1971.

Duensing, Edward and Millmoss, A.B. *The Backyard and Beyond*. Golden, Co: Fulcrum, 1992.

Kulish, John. *Bobcats Before Breakfast*. Harrisburg Pa: Stackpole, 1969.

Rezendez, Paul. *The Wild Within*. Berkley Publishing Group, 1999.

Shepherd, Odell, Editor. *Thoreau's Journals*. New York: Dover, 1961.

Thoreau, Henry David. Thoreau: *A Week on the Concord and Merrimack Rivers; Walden; The Maine Woods; Cape Cod*. New York: Library of America, 1985.

Zajonc, Arthur. *Catching the Light: The Entwined History of Light and Mind*. New York: Oxford University Press, 1993.

Index

Further Reading

Continue your exploration of the natural world
with these titles from Down East Books

The Curious Naturalist
by Sy Montgomery

Award-winning author Sy Montgomery takes readers on an exploratory adventure through the seasons, into the woods, along the seashore, over frozen lakes, and right outside the back door. Paperback, 224 pages.

Wild Things
by Michael McIntosh

This book is devoted to animals native to North America and dear to Michael McIntosh's heart. He is a master essayist, combining natural science, myth, history, poetry, and a lifetime of personal experience. Hardcover, 394 pages, 31 b&w illustrations.

Saving Maine: An Album of Conservation Success Stories
by Bill Silliker Jr.

The primary thrust of this photography album is to answer the question of whether natural Maine is vanishing. The answer is not all of it, thanks to the devoted efforts and generosity of people and conservation groups. Filled with stunning color photographs, this book covers the stories of ten nature preserves or parks created in the state. Hardcover, 96 pages, 80 color photos.

Discovering Moths: Nighttime Jewels in Your Own Back Yard
by John Himmelman

Moths offer an incredible variety of color, form, behavior, and ecological significance, but since most of them are active only at night, we are often simply unaware of them, John Himmelman opens our eyes, showing how moth-watching can offer as much beauty and fascination as birding. Paperback, 240 pages, 50 color and 5 b&w photos, 42 pen and ink illustrations.

Look for them at your favorite bookstore or call
Down East Books at 1-800-685-7962